D0513719

BACK ON THE HOUSE

BACK ON THE HOUSE

Simon Hoggart

Illustrated by John Jensen

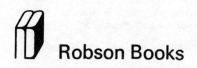

Robson Books

The author and publishers would like to thank the editor and proprietors of *Punch* magazine for permission to reproduce material in this book. Thanks are also owed to the editor and proprietors of the *Guardian*, and to those of the *Observer* for permission to reproduce additional material.

FIRST PUBLISHED IN GREAT BRITAIN IN 1982 BY ROBSON BOOKS LTD., BOLSOVER HOUSE, 5-6 CLIPSTONE STREET, LONDON W1P 7EB.
COPYRIGHT © 1982 SIMON HOGGART

British Library Cataloguing in Publication Data

Hoggart, Simon
    Back on the House.
    1. Debates and debating—Addresses, essays, lectures 2. Great Britain Parliament. House of Commons—Anecdotes facetiae, satire, etc.
    1. Title
    328.41'072'0207   JN550

    ISBN 0-86051-194-4

Printed in Great Britain by Biddles Ltd., Guildford, Surrey

Introduction

My old boss, Ian Aitken, is the Political Editor of the *Guardian*, and the doyen of lobby correspondents. When I first went to work in the slow-twisting maelstrom of Westminster, he gave me a piece of advice which I have always remembered and indeed pass on myself, like a prematurely aged Dutch uncle, to those who have followed. I had written something about Jeremy Thorpe which the then Liberal leader disliked; in fact he disliked it so much that he denounced the article seven or eight times in different interviews. I was new in the job, callow, inexperienced, and terribly dejected by this. I felt sure that Thorpe's antipathy would communicate itself to his colleagues, who would treat me as a pariah, outcast and ignored whenever titillating scoops and items of secret information were being dispersed. Ian assured me that I had nothing whatever to worry about. 'You see,' he said, 'whenever you make one enemy at Westminster, you automatically make 634 friends.'

This statement, like all real wisdom, is not invariably true. I recall that friends of Mr Stan Newens, the left-wing Labour MP for Harlow, who is cursed with a voice resembling Michael Crawford in 'Some Mothers Do Have 'Em', rang to say that Mr Newens had been so hurt by something I had written that real tears had splashed on to his newspaper. Another Labour MP persuaded a friend, a

Cabinet Minister as it happened, to tell me that while he himself did not mind what I had written about him (I had said, quite accurately, that he was the most sycophantic MP in the House), it had brougnt great distress to his aged mother. I felt sorry for the old lady, whom I had no wish to hurt, but had nothing but contempt for a politician who sought to avoid criticism by hiding behind his mother. In any event, the ludicrous conclusion of his whimpering was that no one might be abused in the public prints except unmarried and childless orphans.

But for the most part, politicians take their medicine like men. Even more dispiriting, they frequently appear to enjoy it. Possibly they just like to see their names in print yet again. Perhaps it is connected with the masochism of the English public schools, a phenomenon which sends others into the furtive alleyways of Mayfair and the establishment of Miss Whipplashe.

Often it was those who appeared in the most ridiculous light in Volume I who were most anxious to have their copy signed. Now and again, in the hopes of increasing the sales of the book, I would appear on radio programmes, where I was occasionally asked how I dared to show my face at the Commons. Yet this was never the problem; on the contrary, as soon as MPs realised that I might serve as a conduit for stories they thought damaging to their colleagues, they would seek me out and even (most welcome of all) phone me at home with news of some absurd peccadillo or cretinous misjudgement. If there is one thing which brings us as much pleasure as the humiliation of our enemies, it is the discomfiture of our friends.

Are there limits to what ought to appear in a gossip column? I think so. Clive James despised the Paul Slickeys as those who send people's children 'crying home from school', and the stock reply always was that the tears were caused really by the original infidelity, or drunkenness, or general debauchery. People who aid not wish to read about their own disgraceful behaviour ought to eschew behaving disgracefully.

Up to a point. All of us who work at Westminster know

of affaires and amours, whose participants would far rather they were kept from the public notice; indeed we pass them round covertly, like schoolboys handing on girly magazines behind the teachers' backs. It is my belief that there are fewer of these liaisons than MPs would have us think, yet I see no reason why one should risk the destruction of an entire family for something which has scant bearing on a man's professional ability and competence.

Not that this is entirely a tribute to our magnanimity, for it is also a reflection of the libel laws. In a British court it is almost impossible to prove that the Minister for the Intelligence Services has had his leg across the girl from the Argentine Embassy without producing a photograph, and not always then. And while MPs might be delighted to pass on their colleagues' little canards in the arcane recesses of Annie's Bar, they are unlikely to be so foolish as to repeat the same information from a witness box.

Now and again an MP will feel the need to take the burden of guilt off his shoulders, and, like Winston Churchill II and Mrs Khashoggi, confess. But there is no more pleasure here than there is for the huntsman who sees the fox waving a white handkerchief, only the dull misery of the Churchill family.

It is a good rule of thumb that one ought not to attack a man through his family. Yet some husbands and wives are essential components of their helpmeets; our knowledge of Denis Thatcher and his strikingly vigorous opinions on so many topics is vital to our understanding of his wife. Similarly one cannot comprehend Michael Foot without knowing something about Jill Craigie, or Tony Benn without making at least a brief reconnoitre of Caroline Benn. But suppose one of these couples were to have a promiscuous daughter or an alcoholic son (they don't). I think that would be different.

But a man's incompetence, geniality, stupidity, wit, ambition, intelligence, vanity, sycophancy, deviousness, charm, and all the other tattered rags of humanity with which a politician must cloak himself—all these are fair and reasonable subjects for the political writer's pen. For all their many and often obvious faults, those who sit at Westminster in our interest are a cross-section of us all. Knot-holed and weathered perhaps, but a cross-section nonetheless. If they have any value at all, these small tales tell us a little more about them.

August 1982   Simon Hoggart

WESTMINSTER CAN BE a cruel place for newcomers. There is a celebrated story—possibly even true—about the young chap who had just made his maiden speech. In the tea room afterwards he encountered an elderly member who leaned across and said: 'My boy, that was a Rolls-Royce of a speech!'

The delighted newcomer mentioned this rococo compliment to the next friend he met. His friend told him: 'Oh, he says that to all the new members. What he meant was that you were well-oiled, almost inaudible and carried on for a very, very long time.'

THERE WERE 131 new MPs in this Parliament, and this presents a serious problem for the policemen, door-keepers, messengers and custodians whose job it is to remember all the faces.

One doorkeeper I spoke to has solved the problem by keeping a typed list against which he has written pithy and unflattering descriptions of each new MP. Any new Member who wishes to contact me may learn if he is 'short and ugly', 'stupid-looking', 'tall, thuggish' or 'looks like Engelbert Humperdink'.

LIKE ALL GREAT FEUDS, the continuing antagonism between Margaret Thatcher and Edward Heath feeds upon itself. Consider the tradition of a Conservative Prime Minister holding a reception at Downing Street after each Royal Garden Party for those MPs and their wives who had been at the Palace. Heath was invited to one of the first of Margaret Thatcher's garden parties, and as a matter of course to the Number Ten reception afterwards. Perhaps unusually, even unexpectedly, he decided to go. But it happened that Mrs Thatcher was not actually there. She had, it was explained, an emergency audience with the Queen.

No doubt she had. Perhaps Mr Heath did not mind, perhaps he was pleased, perhaps he didn't even notice. But an awful lot of people did, and another episode in this Campbells and MacDonalds of political rows has been recorded for posterity.

THE PROMOTION OF Harold Lever to the House of Lords recalled the famous story about his rich wife, Diane. This is one of those apocryphal stories which are never actually denied.

Lever is supposed to have been asked: 'Would you still have married your wife if she hadn't had two million pounds?' and he replied, his eyes tender with love, 'I would have married her if she had had only one million pounds!'

Mr Peter Shore was being tipped as a future Leader of the Labour Party long before Jim Callaghan even retired:

MR SHORE'S MIEN has now assumed more gravitas, his speeches have become more sonorous, and his whole bearing has come once again to resemble that of a celebrated war-time Prime Minister. Nevertheless his appearance remains as baggy and unkempt as ever. One of his colleagues has now referred to him unkindly as 'the only Labour MP with a Winston Churchill complex and an Adolf Hitler haircut'.

Political prominence sometimes brings the threat of danger. Arrangements are then made for protection.

ONE VAGUELY IMAGINES that this means squads of secret-service men with bulging pockets and sharp suits, fanning out every time a politician leaves his house to buy a packet of fags. There is some truth in this image, since the detectives do carry guns, but they do no more fanning-out than tap-dancing. Mostly they are highly intelligent policemen, often Cockneys, virtually always members of the Special Branch.

Their main job is intelligence gathering, and they would regard it as a sign of failure to have to shoot somebody. If their man is invited to a dinner party in, say, Northampton, they will assess possible terrorist activity in the area, sift the stream of death threats many leading politicians receive, and so forth. On rare occasions they will advise their man (or woman) not to go. At other times you can spot them sitting disconsolately alone at restaurant tables twenty feet from the gathering being attended by the object of their cares. They drink lemonade while their charge is tossing back the Montrachet.

Some politicians remain on cool, even distant, terms with their protectors. Others positively encourage an easy-going relationship. Gerry Fitt, the brave MP for West Belfast, is one of these. I recall travelling back from a conference at Oxford with Fitt and two of his bodyguards. They were teasing him about his evident hangover that morning.

'We realised you was in a bad way when we come to get you up and you offered us a fiver to get you a cup of tea.'

'Ah dear, boys, I was in a bad way,' said Fitt, explaining that he had made the mistake of drinking whisky instead of gin the previous night.

'Yes,' said the other Special Branch man, 'we realise now why you're a Roman Catholic.'

'Why's that, boys?' asked Fitt.

'Because you get so close to death every time you fall asleep.'

EVERY YEAR, around Christmas, the journalists who work at the Palace of Westminster throw a children's party. As well as their own offspring they generally invite a few dozen deprived children from the Westminster area. For this reason various celebrities are pleased to turn up, and at one recent event these included the, sadly now deceased, Arthur Lowe, Rod Hull with Emu, and Mrs Margaret Thatcher.

She was at her relaxed best. She smiled and chatted with the children and put them all at ease. Everybody seemed happy except for one small four-year-old boy who sat crying into his bowl of dessert. As Mrs Thatcher passed he looked up and said, 'Miss, miss! They've given me blancmange and I don't like blancmange.'

'That,' she said, smiling sweetly, 'is what parties are all about: eating food you don't like!'

This is not a view I have ever heard before, and I think it tells us a lot about her style of government.

12

Mr Nicholas Fairbairn became an early favourite of the column long before his greater fame in the more popular news-papers:

ONE MAN FOR WHOM the sun rises early over the yardarm is Mr Nicholas Fairbairn, the Scottish Tory MP who inherited Lord Home's old seat. On the shuttle flight to London one morning he demanded a drink. Told that no drinks were served on shuttles, he demanded an explanation. When informed that there wasn't a drop of refreshment on board, he astonished the stewardesses by requesting a plastic cup, unscrewing the silver knob off his cane, and pouring out a generous measure of whisky from the interior of the hollow stick.

Every now and then newspapers like to be censorious about House of Commons perks.

ONCE AGAIN the papers are hammering on about how the taxpayers subsidise MPs' food, and the *Daily Mail* has produced a figure of £5.37 per meal. Quite how these sums are conjured up is not clear. Since the annual debt of the Refreshment Department is around two-thirds of a million pounds, and since it provides roughly two-thirds of a million meals every year for the 4,000 people who work at the Commons, the *Mail* figure does seem a little high.

Perhaps as the pampered secretaries, security men, doorkeepers, cleaners, research assistants, electricians, shorthand writers and storemen sit down to their gourmet feasts of sausage and chips, egg and chips, bacon and chips and occasionally, shepherds' pie, they

13

may reflect that if the executives on the *Mail* ate in the firm's canteen every day, their copy each morning might be rather cheaper.

When the House is sitting late, food and drink have to be available to MPs at all hours, sometimes through the night. This is one reason why the Department makes such a loss. During an all-night sitting in the days of the last Labour Government, one right-wing Tory called into the Members' Cafeteria for his breakfast. From the Spanish-speaking waiter, who appeared to be a refugee from Fawlty Towers, a sort of Manuel of the Mountebanks, he ordered porridge and two sausages. Moments later the surprised waiter brought him his order: a bowl of porridge with the two sausages neatly arranged on top.

I HEAR A TOUCHING and delightful story about the Prime Minister. Recently she held a formal dinner party at Chequers, and one of the serving girls accidentally spilled gravy all over Sir Geoffrey Howe's suit. Seeing this disaster, Mrs Thatcher was on her feet immediately. She rushed round the table to comfort, not the Chancellor, but the girl, cuddling her and saying, 'Don't worry, my dear, it could happen to anyone.'

Some of her Ministers are beginning to wonder whether she might show the same spontaneous kindness to them. She has acquired the habit, on meeting them, of making some brisk and derogatory remark, then plunging on her way without even waiting for a servile whimper of apology. One Cabinet Minister almost literally bumped into her the other day. Before he could recover his breath, she remarked: 'Ah, still letting the French walk all over you, I see!'

In his closing days as Defence Secretary, Francis Pym was trying to decide what to do about Sea Eagle, a new British missile which leaps out across the ocean like a porpoise on heat, then levels up and charges at whichever unlucky Communists or South Americans happen to be in its way. The Minister found himself next

to Mrs Thatcher in the voting lobby.

'Ah, Francis,' she said crisply, 'which is that missile that goes . . . ?' and here she made a waving motion with her hand, as if stroking a dromedary's back.

'That would be Sea Eagle, Margaret,' Pym replied, 'I haven't come to a decision about that yet.'

'Well, if you can't make decisions for yourself, Clive and I will have to do it for you. We always do,' she replied, in front of at least half a dozen astonished Tory MPs.

Quite apart from the public rudeness to a very senior Minister, and possible rival, it is not thought wise to call attention to the power and influence wielded by dashing, music-loving, grammar-school educated Clive Whitmore, 46, her Principal Private Secretary. Doubtless he is a splendid fellow in every way, but quite a few MPs suspect he might be getting a little too big for his boots, and incidents like this will not have reassured them.

As for the Prime Minister, she would do well to lay in a small stock of loyalty, like her famous tins of food, against the day when she might be running short.

MRS THATCHER has an excellent capacity to make small talk with important people—voters for example. But in expendable company, say at a social gathering of journalists or backbenchers, she does not muck about. One is greeted with a radiant smile. The hand comes forward. Your mouth finds itself open to make a suitable remark (preferably an ingratiating one, along the lines of 'You certainly got Sterling M3 broadly defined under control last month,' or 'By Jove, Prime Minister, you made Brian Walden look small on Weekend World!').

But no. She has spotted someone more important over your shoulder. Suddenly there is firm pressure on your hand. Your heels gently leave the ground and politely but firmly you are propelled to the other side of the room. It's all so smooth and so quick that you hardly notice it happening, though a 'wet' backbencher I met the other day was still rubbing his sore wrist.

The column paid a couple of visits to Rhodesia, before and after it became Zimbabwe. I was delighted to learn in Salisbury that the Governor Lord Soames, affectionately known as 'Bunter' to his colleagues back in Blighty, was living in the style to which he has for so long been accustomed.

TO THE EXISTING SPLENDOURS of Government House he has added liberal quantities of food and drink (including French wine, which is to all intents and purposes unobtainable in Rhodesia) and the finest fattest Havana cigars. When the Governor tours the country, he goes by Lockheed C-130, or Hercules. Soldiers who are transported in these gigantic, hippo-like planes fly at 250 feet or lower in order to fool any armed guerillas who might be lurking around in the bush beneath. This means that the plane makes a series of juddering and·

nauseating twists, turns, climbs and sweeps leaving even hardened airmen green of face and turbulent in tummy. But the Governor's Hercules takes quite different measures to avoid the heat-seeking SAM missiles. It climbs in a series of spirals above a safe area, and then flies serenely thousands of feet high above the few puffy clouds in the African sky. Here stewards are able to place embroidered table cloths in front of Bunter, to serve him tea and creamy cakes from silver and bone china.

The youngest Soames son, Rupert, aged 20, recently travelled to Salisbury (now called Harare) to visit his father and his delightful mother, the former Mary Churchill. Rupert attended a reception for a group of American congressmen on a fact-finding tour. One of the legislators could be heard dashing across the room to get hold of his wife. 'Honey,' he bellowed, 'I want you to come over here and meet Winston Churchill's *grandson*! Now, what did you say your name was, sonny?'

MR JULIAN AMERY, flagship of the famous 'Dreadnought' class of Tory MP and leading member of the Imperialist Guard, has been telling a topical story about the time in the late Twenties when his father Leo who was, if anything, even more imperialist than his son, took him to see a royal arrival at Victoria station. As the magnificently bedecked figure emerged from the train, a Cockney standing near the Amerys asked his companion who it was.

'Why, that's the King of Arfgarnistan,' the friend replied. The Cockney mused for a moment, then asked, 'Who's King of the other arf, then?'

SINCE THE RT HON Anthony Wedgwood Benn, Viscount Stansgate, whittled his name down to Tony Benn (the next stage must be total proletarianisation, for example Alfie Wedge), I gather that the MP for Ormskirk, also a Labour left-winger, has been growing his. When he was at the LSE he was known as 'Bob Silk'. Now he is addressed as Robert Kilroy-Silk. How much longer will it be if ever he becomes a Minister?

In Spring of 1980, Mr Roy Mason faced one of the periodic attempts, led by Mr Arthur Scargill, to deprive him of his seat in Barnsley.

I WOULD BE SORRY to see Mr Roy Mason ousted, if only because it would deprive the Commons of one man's extraordinary obsession. In the way that some build endless model railways, or the Taj Mahal from matchsticks, Mr Mason designs neckties. He will design a tie for anything—an election, a club, an institution, a friend recovering from piles, almost anything at all. Recently he designed a tie to commemorate Annie's Bar, that Rover's Return of the Commons where the more bibulous hacks and legislators can buy each other drinks and trade confidences. The tie, available in Tory blue, Labour red, or neutral green, has the Commons portcullis badge (which is, quaintly enough, actually a watergate), the word 'Annie's' in a vertical scroll arrangement, and what looks like a cauliflower in a pot, but which turns out to be a foaming mug of beer.

Shortly before the election, Mr Mason was in New York trying to persuade American businessmen dense enough to listen, or grasping enough to take the huge grants on offer, to set up shop in Northern Ireland, whose Secretary of State he then was. Mr Mason had some success in this line, and signed up Mr John de Lorean at a cost of many tens of millions of pounds to the taxpayer.

One of his senior civil servants found himself eating a hamburger opposite a man who was evidently a visitor to Gotham City. This was apparent because he was wearing a wide-brimmed hat and a massive, multi-coloured tie

made from a fabric not usually found in nature. It proclaimed vividly: 'Hi, I'm from Texas.'

After a while the man leaned across, and said, 'Say, I collect neckties, and I never saw one like you're wearing. Willya tell me about it?' The civil servant drew himself up to his full height and said, 'This tie was designed by Her Majesty's Principal Secretary of State for Northern Ireland to commemorate the successful and safe visit of Queen Elizabeth to the province on the occasion of her Silver Jubilee in August 1977.'

'Wow!' said the Texan, 'that's fantastic. You know if I had a tie like that it would be the greatest thing in my collection.'

The civil servant reached towards his collar. 'Fella,' he said in the vernacular, 'you just got lucky.' Two minutes later he walked out of the restaurant for his next meeting with Mr Mason wearing a tie labelled 'Hi, I'm from Texas.'

IT IS NOT commonly known about David Owen that he proposed to his lovely wife Debbie by telephone. Which proves that there is nothing, absolutely nothing, which will persuade a modern doctor to make a house call.

One optimistic prediction turned out to be very true:

ROWS IN THE Labour Party are not what they were. In the Fifties, left and right did not merely disagree; they loathed each other in a way which made the Montagues and Capulets look like a swingers' circle. Not only did they refuse to talk to each other, but would spread the most vicious and vituperative gossip wherever a willing ear could be found. Even an unwilling one would do. The great and sonorous issues, such as German rearmament and nationalisation, were swiftly reduced to mere clashes of personality. The poison was so powerful that it infected people more or less on the same side, so that Attlee disliked Morrison intently, and plenty of people, including a few Bevanites, couldn't stand Bevan.

Sadly these days appear, at the moment, to have gone. It's possible to see people on opposite sides of the party drinking in the same bar, perhaps even arguing in an amicable kind of way. People make remarks like 'I may disagree with his politics, but he's a bloody good lad all the same.' It's terribly dull.

However, there are some hopeful signs that the days of hatred and bitterness may be returning to beguile us. Merlyn Rees, as Home Secretary, used to give delightful dinner parties in the magnificent surroundings of Dorney Wood, Buckinghamshire, a stately home of modern construction which is reserved for the use of senior Ministers. There was good food, good wine, good conversation and croquet on the lawns by way of an aperitif. Not long ago Mr and Mrs Rees made the unusual mistake of inviting both the left-wing Neil Kinnocks and the very right-wing William Rodgerses, still in the Labour Party. Soon Neil Kinnock was in a furious argument with Bill Rodgers, and Sylvia Rodgers soon in an equally acrimonious dispute with Glenys Kinnock.

Shortly after the meal was over, Mrs Kinnock, who had been looking round the house, stood at the top of the stairs and heard the Reeses asking sadly: 'Do you really have to go so soon?' Mrs Rodgers replied, 'We'd love to stay longer but we can't stand any more of those Kinnocks!' Being a woman of discretion, Glenys tiptoed quietly out of earshot. The great days of passion and loathing may soon be back.

A *PUNCH* READER writes to me from Hong Kong to say that the name of Ian Gow, Mrs Thatcher's Parliamentary Private Secretary, known to one and all as 'Supergrass', translated into Chinese characters, is the same as the word for the male organ. He is looking forward to the newspaper reports: 'Mrs Thatcher, accompanied by . . .'

Tory party conferences never disappoint.

DOWN AT THE grass roots there are still women with gigantic single-breasted bosoms, floral dresses the size of chintz-covered sofas, hats like the domes on Byzantine churches and voices that could cut a diamond at fifty yards. The men wear great shaggy sports jackets, resembling lovat-coloured mammoths, and those massive brown brogues covered in little holes, as if fashioned from a bison with acne. Now and again you bump into some aristocrat named after a place abolished by Peter Walker. Recently I mumbled an apology to one such, and saw that his plastic name-tag carried in huge letters 'The Duke of Rutland'.

A colleague and I were filing past the police barrier to reach the conference hall. Across the barrier various people were handing out leaflets to the delegates and shouting slogans. One woman was from a pressure group which tries to help children in poverty. She asked, 'Will any of you spend just five minutes finding out what happens to children who don't have nannies, au pairs or boarding schools?' The middle-aged man behind me said grumpily 'People shouldn't have children if they can't look after them.'

I liked the story told by John Watson, the agreeable Tory MP for Skipton. His seven-year-old son Alexander and his class were asked to write a letter to God. A pretty silly idea, if you ask me, but Alexander did fine. He wrote to his Maker: 'Dear God, how come you are never on the telly? My daddy is sometimes on the telly, and he is not half as famous as you.' This composition got four out of ten, 'not long enough'.

LABOUR MP Mr Neville Sandelson's headlong rush towards oblivion, urged over the cliff by his left-wing constituency party, like a sort of Jonathan Livingston Lemming, continues apace. I have recorded his reaction to a letter from his local party, Hayes and Harlington, which complained that he was never working at the House of Commons when they wanted to see him. Sandelson took the letter from his pigeonhole at the House, read it, scrawled 'Not Known At This Address' on the envelope, and sent it back. Another letter, from an angry constituency official, was signed with the man's surname and only the initials of his forenames. Sandelson, though he knew the fellow perfectly well, began his reply: 'Dear Sir or Madam.'

From time to time the House erupts into what is later described as a 'riot'. Not surprisingly they involve Parliament's most colourful figures.

ONE'S SYMPATHY FOR Mr Nicholas Fairbairn, the Government Minister who was jostled by Labour MPs during pugnacious scenes in the Commons, is limited. Mr Fairbairn can look after himself, and his anxious constituents may be reassured: he will recover from his Night of Terror.

The fact is that Thursday's rowdy scenes were a miserable skirmish, a mere pillow-fight, compared to the open warfare which has been carried on in the Commons during previous years. Even the red lines woven into the carpet a few feet before each front bench recall those days. MPs on their feet are not allowed to step beyond the lines, which are drawn two swords' lengths from each other. They reflected the real danger that an angry member might attempt to run an opponent through.

There is an engraving of the fist fight in the Commons over the Home Rule Bill in 1893. There are at least two dozen members actively engaged in the punch-up, smashing each other in the face, grabbing at each other's clothing, and generally behaving in a manner which would be thought lacking in etiquette in Glasgow at closing time.

This was an extreme example of a fairly common occurrence. In 1661, Pepys thought the young men who sat in Parliament were 'the most profane swearing fellows that I ever heard in my life, which makes me think they will spoil all, and bring things into a warr if they can'. Dickens, probably the most distinguished parliamentary corres-pondent the place has ever seen, said it offered more noise and confusion than anywhere else he knew, 'not excepting Smithfield on a market day, or a cockpit in all its glory'.

Mr Fairburn's remarks about 'mob rule' were fore-shadowed a hundred and fifty years ago by Hazlitt, who remarked that few people who had distinguished themselves in the Commons had ever done anything else.

Such riots have their own traditions, as rigid in their way as those surrounding other parliamentary customs. For instance, at one point the Speaker generally says something along these lines: 'I want to tell the House we are endangering our parliamentary principles. What has happened tonight is quite unprecedented.'

These words were used by Speaker Thomas on this occasion. He was quite wrong. Such scenes are no more unprecedented than Halley's Comet, and a great deal more frequent.

In 1931 when Mr John McGovern, the Labour MP for Glasgow Shettleston, refused to sit down when told to do so by the Speaker, the Serjeant at Arms approached him and tried to persuade him otherwise. Mr McGovern swore at him. Then six of the Serjeant's aides came to carry him off. He took them all on. One was cracked on the head, another winded, and a third had his shin bruised.

Then the real fight began. Four other Red Clydesiders plunged into the fray and attacked the attendants as if in a rugby scrum. The attendants managed to get hold of Mr McGovern and carried him horizontally from the Chamber. The Labour MP John Beckett attempted another tackle on one of the attendants, missed, and crashed to the floor.

Nor are these simply memories of a bygone age when people were more passionate and hot-tempered than the calm, professional legislator of today. On average, I'd guess, the sitting has to be suspended by the Speaker once a year because MPs are making too much noise for business to continue. The late Tom Swain, a mining MP, thumped a Tory who had displeased him, in full view of the Speaker. Another Labour MP once bopped Mr Neil Kinnock in the face because of something he thought he had said.

In 1972 Bernadette Devlin slapped the Home Secretary, and pulled his hair, in protest against the death of thirteen innocent people in Londonderry on Bloody Sunday. There was the CS gas incident when a young Ulsterman called Bowes Egan hurled a canister on to the floor of the House. In 1978 Dom Mintoff's daughter, Yana, flung animal dung at MPs in the Chamber—again, a protest over Ireland. In 1976 Mr Heseltine, incensed by a narrow vote won by the Labour Government and the subsequent chorus of the Red Flag from the Labour benches, seized the Commons mace and swung it round his head, so earning himself the sobriquet 'Tarzan' and a lifetime reputation for being rather silly.

People are always complaining that standards in the Chamber have declined. They are, perhaps sadly, wrong. Incidents like these may be distressing for the Speaker and those caught up in them. But they are as time-encrusted and traditional as the old place itself.

I RAN INTO a couple of Tory MPs discussing the witty and vehement attack made on the Government by Michael Edwardes of BL. 'It takes some guts to kick a man in the goolies when you're about to ask for another £1,000 millions,' one of them mused. 'Aha,' replied the other, 'in Keith he has chosen the one Minister whose reaction would be to apologise because his goolies had got in the way of your foot.'

TED HEATH'S bitter denunciation of Mrs Thatcher's politics are yet another reminder of the sheer depth of his dislike for the woman. I recall vividly one of those dramatic little scenes which somehow epitomise an emotion or a state of mind more than any speech or phrase could do.

It was in March 1979, the Labour Government had just lost the crucial confidence vote. Jim Callaghan had announced the election, and the Conservatives seemed the almost certain winners. An air of near-manic jubilation could be detected in the lobbies and the Smoking Room. In the Conservative whips' office, the first bottles of champagne were being unpopped.

Ted Heath walked slowly away from the Lobby, a look of resigned gloom on his face, like Sidney Carton with toothache. A Tory whip rushed up behind him, tapped him on the shoulder, and said, 'Ted, come for a drink with us!' Heath slowly shook his head and walked on. 'Just this once, this one time,' pleaded the Whip, but Heath did not break step, moving slowly through the sounds of revelry, alone towards his office.

In the manner of a Buckingham Palace spokesman apologising for Princess Anne, one of Heath's assistants later told me that he had not realised at the time that Mrs Thatcher would be present at the piss-up. I wonder. He was certainly as glum as I have ever seen him.

MR FOOT'S CHOICE of front bench spokesmen reflects his deep belief in the virtues of self-educated men. Take, for example, Mr Frank McElhone, who, rather to everybody's surprise, found himself the Shadow Minister for Overseas Development.

Mr McElhone was the winner in an informal contest between Labour MPs to discover the most revolting thing which had happened in any of their constituencies. The conversation covered the odd pit disaster, the occasional accident with machinery at a local factory, a nasty suicide and so forth. Then Mr McElhone, whose seat includes the Gorbals district of Glasgow, silenced everybody with his tale.

A constituent of his had murdered his wife and had decided to dispose of the body by carving it up on the kitchen table. This task had proved more difficult than he had expected, and so after making a perfunctory attempt to sever the odd limb, he had pushed the body into a sack, heaved it over his back and set off down the tenement stairs towards the canal. Halfway down the street, however, an arm had worked loose. A passing dog, seeing and smelling it, had leapt up and grabbed the arm, running off down the street. A dog with a severed human arm in its mouth is an unusual sight, even in Glasgow, and the incident caused the man to be arrested directly. Not surprisingly, nobody could top this story.

Mr McElhone, though one of the most charming MPs at Westminster, is not famous for his laconic taciturnity. So great is his enthusiasm for whatever subject he takes up that it is sometimes a difficult task to divert him. Not long ago I remember a colleague and myself discussing with him the topic of race relations in Scotland. These owing to the more or less total absence of coloured immigrants north of the border, are generally good. My colleague pointed out, however, the true fact that a number of Asians have set up shops in the Western Isles. Here amid the crofts, the wiry grass, the slow, ruminative cattle and the wild keening of the gulls, one may buy Indian groceries, poppadums, curious dark spices and exotically shaped vegetables. Was this so? inquired Frank. Indeed it was, my colleague said. In fact they had made a film about one of these shopkeepers. Frank expressed great interest. It was, my colleague pressed on, about a Pakistani greengrocer who had run out of supplies because bad weather had prevented the ferry crossing from the mainland. Perhaps Mr McElhone (then a Minister in the Scottish Office) had seen it? No, he replied. How strange, said the colleague, because it was very well known. It was titled *Last Mango On Harris*. I have never seen Frank shut up so quickly.

A GROVELLING APOLOGY appeared in the New Year *Border Telegraph*, a paper which serves south-eastern Scotland and the parliamentary seat represented by Mr David Steel. The apology contained the entire text of Mr Steel's less than thrilling New Year message to his constituents. It explained that because of a typographic mistake, the message had been jumbled with that sent in by the Duke of Buccleuch, who is the Big Cheese of the Borders. Mr Steel's message had therefore seemed to begin: 'I am overjoyed and delighted that this has been a year of economic gloom and despondency.'

A STORY ABOUT the thick Irish, balanced by one about the thick British. When Mrs Thatcher took three of her senior Ministers for important talks in Dublin, it was decided at the last minute that they ought to split into two groups and fly in separate planes. The idea was to avoid the shattering effect on our national morale if the Prime Minister, the Foreign Secretary, the Ulster Secretary and the Chancellor were to disappear simultaneously in one blazing aircraft. So, at an expense certainly more than £20,000, another Andover was prepared, a crew briefed, flight plans filed, and away the two parties zoomed. The moment the planes put down, both groups were rushed into a single Irish Army helicopter which took them for the last and most perilous portion of their journey. Now a more damaging story. Don Concannon, the Labour MP who is Northern Ireland spokesman for this party, became an Ulster Minister in the Callaghan government some years ago. All Irish Ministers are immediately allotted security protection from the Special Branch. Concannon gave the authorities his address, Flat 6B in a street I won't name.

For a month and a half he would come and go, and never once saw any burly men standing in the street peering over the garden wall. Concannon was much impressed by their skills and discretion, and felt far safer knowing that such highly-trained professionals were watching over him night and day.

After this period there was a knock on the door. When he opened it a large Special Branch gentleman said, 'Is this number 6B? Thank God for that, for the past six weeks we've been staking out number 68.'

MR ROY JENKINS'S political instincts are not, I fear, invariably altogether reliable. A while ago, while he was still sitting in the Commons as a Labour MP, he was canvassing support for something or other, and expressed the worry that he was not all that well known among his colleagues. Why, he asked, did he not have more support?

A Welsh colleague explained that people thought him—unfairly perhaps, for Mr Jenkins is an exceedingly pleasant and convivial man—a trifle stand-offish. He ought to make more of his Welshness, chat to people make them feel that he saw them as equals. Take old so-and-so, he said, naming a particularly ancient Welsh MP, he'd be your friend for life if you simply greeted him warmly and bought him a drink. Why, he added, you'll find him in the Strangers' Bar now.

So Jenkins popped off and there indeed the old gaffer was. 'Good to see you, Dai' (or Ivor, or Evan, or whatever the chap's name happened to be). 'What can I buy you to drink?'

'Why, that's very generous of you, Roy,' said the MP in some surprise, 'I'll take a pint of bitter, if you don't mind.'

'Certainly, one pint of bitter coming up,' said the genial former Chancellor.'I'm terribly sorry I can't join you, as I've got an urgent appointment, but it's been very pleasant to see you.'

So saying, he strolled off leaving the elderly member to drink his beer alone and to reflect on the way in which the tide of history is changed not by great events but by trivial traits of personality.

NOTED TORY WET MP Richard Needham of Chippenham tells me of an intriguing encounter in his constituency. Chippenham is famous for few things, but it is known throughout the world as the place where, following a fatal road crash, the famous rock and roll singer Eddie Cochran left to join the choir invisible. There is some controversy in Chippenham about whether a memorial to Mr Cochran should be put up in the town. Mr Needham, a great aficionado of the music of the period, is keen that this should be done, and agreed to appear on a local TV programme to say so.

With great excitement Needham and the crew tracked down the now aged man who had been first on the scene of the crash. Yes, he told them, he had been there. Yes, he had seen it happen. Yes, he had given what help he could and yes, he would tell everything on the programme. Lights and sound equipment were prepared, the gentleman posed on the appropriate chalk mark, directional mikes and wind baffles suspended out of the shot, and the senior citizen began talking. 'Yes, oy was there,' he said. 'Oy rushed out and saw them lying all over the road. Oy put moy coat over Eddie Cochran. Oy never got it back.'

ANOTHER STORY ABOUT Tina—the acronym for 'There Is No Alternative'. Recently the directors of the giant GEC company were making arrangements to receive her on an official visit. They rang Number Ten to say that they had thought of omitting one particular plant from the tour since it would necessitate wearing protective clothing. Would the Prime Minister mind? 'Not in the slightest,' came the airy answer from Downing Street. 'She just *loves* dressing up!'

A SPLENDID EXAMPLE of how Mr Whitelaw copes with TV interviews, especially in the occasional circumstances of his not having the faintest idea of what he is talking about.

He was being interviewed 'down the line' by Tyne-Tees television about the closure of an iron foundry in his constituency. The interviewer, who was in Newcastle, had been well-briefed, and reeled off a series of impressive statistics: the number of jobs lost, the unemployment ratio in the constituency, the relevant investment grants and so forth.

Willie, who was in a studio in London, clearly had not a clue about any aspect of the closure. After each crisp and well-informed question he would go 'hmm, well, yes, harrumph' until the interviewer was obliged to start talking again. Then, after this had gone on for five minutes, he suddenly and unexpectedly developed a terrible coughing fit. This continued for fully 30 seconds, an eternity in television time. Willie made more and more noise, his face went purple, and it seemed for one horrendous moment that the Home Secretary might expire in the studio. Luckily the interview was being taped, so they were able to start again from scratch.

This time he was dazzling. 'I'm so glad you asked me that. I gather that this closure will mean the loss of four hundred jobs, it brings the rate of unemployment in the area up to 21 per cent, but investment grants are available . . .' He went on until he had repeated back at the interviewer every fact he had learned the first time. At this point, the line to Newcastle was cut, and this reply, redolent with sympathy, compassion and a profound knowledge of all the crucial figures, was the one which Tyne-Tees were obliged to broadcast.

POOR SIR GEOFFREY HOWE will no doubt draw great encouragement through the difficult months ahead from his deputy at the Treasury, Mr Leon Brittan. Mr Brittan, the Tory MP for Cleveland and Whitby, is also the brother of Mr Sam Brittan, the celebrated, right-wing economic thinker. It was Sam who had the kindly thought of laying on a reception when Leon got married. (Incidentally, he married a constituent who had been married to someone else when he first met her, which shows how much times have changed in the Tory party.)

Sam engaged a butler whose job it was to serve the drinks. Before the guests arrived, this flunky was in place at the luxurious Holland Park residence, polishing glasses.

'Here,' he said, 'are you the Samuel Brittan I read about in the *Guardian*, who's a supporter of this Milton

Friedman bloke?'

'Yes,' said Sam, with quiet pride, 'I suppose so. We disagree on certain points of course, but broadly speaking I'd say that I agree with him.'

'In that case,' the butler said, 'you're no better than Hitler.' With that he stormed out, leaving the new Chief Secretary, the bride and guests to pour out their own champagne.

IT WOULD BE a mistake to say that the late Frank Maguire, the Independent MP for Fermanagh and Tyrone, was an enormously popular man. For a start, few people at Westminster knew him. He must have turned up in London half a dozen times in the seven years he served as an MP. He was far better known for the many (no doubt apocryphal) stories which were told about him. Allegedly on one recent visit, he asked a policeman why the flags in Whitehall were at half-mast, and was told 'The old Duke of Gloucester's gone, sir.'

'Very sad,' said Maguire, 'mind you I never drank there myself.' I don't think I believe that, nor the legend that he didn't know how to buy a tube ticket. It's said that he heard the woman in front of him say 'Maida Vale, single,' and so said boldly 'Frank Maguire, married.' It is certainly true that he made a special trip to Westminster in 1979 for the Confidence vote which brought down the Labour Government, in order that he might, as he put it, 'abstain in person'.

Throughout the Labour administration, the government kept a supply of Catholic whips of Irish descent whose job it was to phone Maguire at crucial times when every vote was needed. Once, during a particularly bloody time in Northen Ireland, they phoned the bar he ran in his constituency, and his wife answered. She promised to pass on their request, but warned that she didn't want her husband in London 'with all those bombs going off'. He was a most agreeable man. I once overheard part of a long and affable conversation he held over several drinks with a friend of mine. Frank ended by

after SHARAKU

saying how very much he had enjoyed their chat. 'Tell me, Chris,' he said, 'will you be here tomorrow?'

'Certainly,' Chris replied.

'Ah dear, what a pity. You see I shan't be,' Maguire ended.

I HAVE A NEW Willie Whitelawism. The Home Secretary was giving evidence to a House of Commons Select Committee examining the overcrowding in Britain's prisons. Willie made his position absolutely clear on this urgent issue. 'I can assure you that I definitely might take action,' he said.

THE DECISION BY the Social Democrats to allow people to send subscriptions and gifts by means of credit cards gives a new meaning to the old Labour party idea of a card vote. Card votes are always on contentious issues, and are the occasions when the great trade unions put in their hundreds of thousands of votes for or against some motion or other. They are the reason why a hall containing no more than two thousand people can produce a majority of five million or so.

Presumably at Social Democrat conferences they will have credt card votes. 'For the motion, Barclaycard, 1,250,000 votes, Access 975,000. Against, Diners Club, 630,000, Harrods Charge Account, 24,000. I declare the motion carried. . . .' People will rise and cry: 'On a point of order, Mr Chairman!'

'Who do you represent?'

'American Express, Mr Chairman.'

'That will do nicely.'

By June of 1981, the New US President was well entrenched.

PRESIDENT REAGAN IS now, 12 weeks after he was shot, one of the most popular leaders America has had since the Second World War. His advisers are already talking about a second term, which means that he would quit the job at the age of 78. Last week one Congressman I met said: 'What scares me is that this man is so popular that he could announce a nuclear war, and everyone would say "That's just great, Mr President".'

One secret is his remarkable relaxation. Americans call it being 'laid back', though a closer English translation might be 'lying down'. His team said that when they took office they would 'hit the the ground running', which they certainly have. Reagan himself hit the ground fast asleep.

Jimmy Carter used to get up at 5 am. Reagan's chief aides don't meet until 7.30, when the President is still snoozing. He turns up around 8.45 most days and, after a tough morning's decision-taking, goes back for a nap. If it's a working afternoon, which it often isn't, he'll be back in the Residence at six for some much-needed rest before facing a strenuous reception or dinner party. Then he's back home to greet the Sandman for the final visit of the day.

This hectic schedule has, of course, had to be toned down since the attempts on his life. He doesn't, for example, work quite so many afternoons, but the basic outline remains the same. It always has. During the election campaign, the hours between one and three were euphemistically listed as 'staff time'. It became quite a popular phrase. Mothers would call their children in of an evening, saying 'c'mon honey, it's staff time'.

He is the first man for 20 years to make the Presidency a part-time job, a means of filling up a few of the otherwise blank days of retirement

There is no evidence that the American people mind this. Reagan came to power promising to get the Government off the backs of the people and he has begun with himself, getting on to his own back instead. Carter behaved like the school swot, who had to know everything and to read every memo and every briefing. He even used to read the list of people using the White House tennis court each day. Reagan, by contrast, doesn't read much at all. Memos to him are short and give the general gist of an argument or a position. Details are left to other people.

I called in at a Reagan press conference to see at first hand the technique of government by somnambulism. It was fascinating. No British politician would dare to try it.

It was only the third press conference he has held since coming to office in January. Carter had one every fortnight for his first two years. One of those firm yet oily voices which sounds as if its owner gargled with a dry Martini every morning announced 'Ladies and Gentlemen, the President of the United States!', and we all stood up.

Reagan himself looked a little shy, even unsure of himself, as if not quite certain why all these people were here. First he read out a statement which had clearly been , written for him about the necessity of tax cuts. Some Congressional committees, he said sternly, were trying to get around the cuts. One committee had agreed to cut suppers at day care centres but had decreed that lunches could be served instead at supper time. This, he said, using a favourite word of the new administration, was 'unconscionable', which I suppose it is, unless you rely on the free meals.

The whole statement sounded uncharacteristically tough. The true Reagan emerged in the later questions. His most frequent answer, employed three times, was 'Well, I don't really have the answer to that.' There's no way you can harry a man who simply admits that he doesn't know.

The folksiness can get a trifle wearing. At one press conference he was asked a fairly hostile question about the effects of his policies on the poor. He asked, 'How can you say that about a sweet guy like me?' Another time he was asked if he had a message for the Russians. He replied: 'Roses are red, Violets are blue, Stay out of Poland, And El Salvador too.'

This kind of sophisticated global thinking has made some people wonder exactly what the administration's foreign policy is, so last week he took the opportunity to fill us in. 'I am satisfied,' he announced, 'that we do have a foreign policy. Already I have met eight heads of state and the representatives of nine other nations.' This, of course, scarcely amounts to a foreign policy, but then politicians the world over confuse meeting people with taking action.

When he was asked about his health, he looked genuinely pleased that someone should be interested. We inquired about gun control. Well, it turned out that he had had a 'very nice talk' with Senator Kennedy on this very topic. Did we know that there were some 20,000 gun control laws in the various states, and that some of the toughest were right here in the District of Columbia? But they hadn't stopped a fellow in the Hilton Hotel. This is no kind of answer, of course, but no one picked him up on it. You don't shout about at such kindly gents, whether they have come in to help with the gardening or are President of the United States.

This general air of a loveable old grandpop is carried into all his dealings. I talked to two people who had had separate meetings with him recently. One, a Democrat,

REAGAN?

after SHARAKU

said: 'The guy is really dumb. There are a whole lot of questions you ask him, and he does not know the answer. He has to be told.' The other man, a conservative, found him 'most impressive. He was full of jokes and anecdotes about the old Hollywood, and he put us completely at ease. We asked him a bunch of policy questions; some he answered very fully. Others he'd say, "I don't really know about this, but Ed does" and Ed would talk. You came away thinking "the guy's alright".'

'Ed' is Edward Meese III, the White House counsellor, and one of the three or four most powerful men in America. He is the most important of the 'triumvirate' who quite simply are the Presidency during the long hours that Reagan is in bed. Meese has been with Reagan since the 1960s, when he joined him as legal secretary to the Governor of California. His views on almost everything, from the Communist menace to the urban poor, match Reagan's exactly.

His greatest passion is law enforcement. His idea of relaxing is to curl up at home with a good book and the police radio blasting out. Meese is powerful because he not only has the ear of the President, as and whenever the President is awake, but because two of the most powerful offices in the White House—the National Security Council and the Office of Policy Development (basically foreign and home affairs)—report to him.

The next most powerful man to Meese is James A. Baker III (these American dynasties seem to stop at IV; you never meet someone called Frank N. Furter XXVI). Baker's title is Chief of Staff, and he is nominally in charge of staff and organisation. In fact, he also works on policy, where his opinions are especially valuable, because he is one of the tiny handful of people who actually understand how Washington works. It was Baker who persuaded Reagan to lift the Soviet grain embargo just in time to get votes from the farming states for the budget. His reputation was made during the televised debates with Carter. Baker handed the candidate a small card marked 'chuckle', and when Carter began criticising, Reagan chuckled and said 'There you go again.' Amazingly, this was thought to be the key, brilliant answer of the campaign.

The third of the Big Three is Michael Deaver, who has no Roman numerals at all after his name and is thought to be the least significant. But he is a close friend of the Reagan family and is trusted, even loved, by both Reagan and Nancy. He manages the little details, some of them extremely little. For example, Vice-President George Bush changes his watch strap to match his suit. During the campaign, Deaver kept a small supply of straps to offer him. His greatest success was in keeping Reagan politically alive and in front of the public between the end of his years as Governor and the Presidential campaigns.

The point about the Triumvirate is that, unlike Nixon's Haldeman and Erlichman, they are exceedingly nice. People seem to like them and to trust them, though whether they will when things start to get rough, remains to be seen. Already some of the hardline right-wingers are beginning to grumble that Reagan is being led astray from the true path by his more pragmatic advisers. This is the familiar sound of extremists the world over getting ready to complain 'our policies didn't fail; they were never tried'.

One man who has already complained about softness in the arteries is Reagan's ultra-conservative Assistant for Political Affairs, Lyn Nofziger, a monstrous man with a beer belly fashioned from Bombay gin, if so appalling an anatomical formation can be conceived. Nofziger has been with Reagan for fifteen years and said of him during the campaign: 'He is as easily managed as anyone . . . he's not a guy to get mixed up with details. He knows his role.'

Nofziger, who is not a social friend of the Reagans ('they don't drink enough'), is what is called in Washington 'a Movement conservative' which means basically, that he can be trusted by other conservatives. Reagan is very right wing, but that isn't the same thing.

Nofziger is one of his 'lightning rods'; the tough, mean men who take the unpleasant decisions and deflect public unpopularity from their boss. Reagan looks as if every one cent cut in social security payments actually causes him pain; Nofziger enjoys it.

Perhaps the most exotic figure in the Cabinet is Mr James Watt, who is Secretary of the Interior. This means principally that he is in charge of 548 million acres of public lands: parks, coastline and wilderness. Having Watt to run your parks is a little like getting Jack the Ripper to run a Home for Distressed Gentewomen. He is fundamentalist Christian who starts every day with a prayer meeting for his staff.

At one recent meeting Watt was pushing his usual line, which is to allow the banks and the mining companies to rip open America's most beautiful country and get out the minerals and oil. Someone said: 'But if they go ahead with this, there won't be much left for our grandchildren.' Watt replied, 'I don't think we're going to to be around that long. Jesus is coming soon.'

In the Lord's absence, Watt believes, it is mankind's job to get at those minerals which He thoughtfully left in the land. For some years the Lord worked through an organisation called the Mountain States Legal Foundation of which Watt was president. The MSLF fought every conservationist and environmental pressure group and law, with considerable success. Now he has fired every preservationist in his department, and cut $3,000 million off environment programmes.

Watt is pure Reaganism, undiluted and unconfused by any diffident amiability or desire to see the other man's point of view. The outlook is simple: big business is always right because it creates the wealth. Anything, such as taxes and government restrictions, which gets in the way of big business prevents wealth from being created and is, incidentally, against God's law. If, as Watt often does, you can go into a closet, commune with your Maker, and emerge to announce His decision, it is difficult to argue with you.

Reagan himself is a committed right-winger who came to office determined to alter the whole structure of the American economy and American society. Yet the easy-going nature which made him so popular with the voters also means that he is perfectly capable of ignoring the right wing's writ at any time. This gives his ideological backers who at last thought they had their own man in the White House occasional pause for thought. A member of the Heritage Foundation, an ultra-right think tank, told me: 'One question is, will Reagan allow himself to become Thatcherised and start raising taxes rather than cutting them?'

One highly placed official who admires Reagan greatly said: 'For the first time since Eisenhower, we have a President who is not driven by a terrible demon inside himself. He doesn't have to prove anything to anybody. We're actually working with a guy who doesn't mind the fact that he is sometimes wrong, and I cannot tell you what a relief that is.'

CONSERVATIVES, OR AT LEAST a certain type of Conservative, are highly suspicious of all bills to do with animals. I think they suspect that any piece of legislation, whether it is meant to end vivisection or protect some endangered species such as the natterjack toad, is in some subtle way a stalking horse, a harbinger of the bill which one day will seek to abolish fox hunting. Even bills which are concerned purely with looking after the wildlife of the countryside are regarded with extreme wariness, since it is almost inevitable that such an act will interfere with the God-given right to blaze away at anything that has four legs or feathers. For this reason many Tories have been making anxious inquiries about the Laboratory Animals Protection Bill which has been going through the Lords, and have been delighted to learn that it will almost certainly not emerge in the Commons and has, therefore, virtually no chance of becoming law.

This general attitude was exemplified by Lord Thorneycroft who, some time ago, received a letter from Lord Houghton, one of the doughtiest champions of the entire animal kingdom. Houghton sent the Tory chairman a closely-typed, ten-page letter outlining his massive campaign to Put Animals Into Politics. The reply was a polite but remarkably brief letter from Thorneycroft which read: 'Dear Douglas, Thank you for your letter about animals. I do think that the poor creatures have enough to put up with without being put into politics. Yours sincerely . . .'

THE FOREST OF DEAN is a strange and mysterious place. For one thing it is Britain's only working-class forest. In Sherwood or the New Forest one senses aristocratic hunting parties jingling through, occasionally passing furtive charcoal burners or sullen cottagers. They, of course, vote the way that the landowners vote; they judge rightly that the Labour Party threatens the immemorial, melancholy peace of their chosen way of life. But if you drive through the Forest of Dean, along the wide avenues which penetrate its deep brown undergrowth, you will suddenly come upon a council estate, complete with a glum and unpleasant pub, a Spar mini-market, graffiti-covered bus shelters and children with the thin legs which betoken not getting quite enough to eat. It is as if a tornado, rushing through Sheffield or Cardiff some time in the Fifties, had lifted the entire community and deposited it in these baffling and impenetrable woods.

All this is to introduce a note of warning for Mr Paul Marland, a farmer and company director, who in 1979 managed the unusual feat of winning for the Conservatives the seat of Gloucestershire West, which includes the Forest of Dean. A loyal Tory, he gave wholehearted support to the Forestry Bill—indeed followed the bidding of his Whips throughout the wrangles of the Committee Stage. The Bill, however, empowers the Government to sell off ad lib large chunks of Forestry Commission land, and created slow but later monumental anger among the sylvan socialists of the Forest of Dean. They demanded a public meeting with the hapless Marland, a meeting at which they created such uproar that he was obliged to ask for quiet, in order to explain the Bill 'in terms which the ladies might understand'. The uproar from the ladies at this insult almost brought the meeting to an end.

The chastened member tried to bring in a last-minute amendment to exclude the Forest of Dean when the Bill had its Report Stage and Third Reading a week or so ago. He failed and the Forest has returned to its normal state of timeless bucolic resentment. The foresters, however, if asked, point out that Mr Marland is the first Conservative MP they have had for some sixty-three years and, we are assured, the last.

ANOTHER CLUE HAS come my way, casting further light on Denis Healey's defeat in the Labour leadership election. What Healey never did—and it was much resented—was to confide anything to his Junior Ministers or colleagues, with the exception of his Chief Secretary, the tiny Joel Barnett. A Minister from the last Labour government told me that in the end, in order to get some faint idea of what was going on in the Treasury, the junior economics Ministers actually joined together to invite their burly boss to lunch. 'Even then he didn't come,' the former Minister told me.

I SEE THAT Mrs Frances Morrell has become deputy boss of the Inner London Education Authority. Mrs Morrell, who is best known as Mr Tony Benn's political adviser (a fact which did not figure on her election address) is now clearly on her way. We can expect to hear much more of her.

Opinion at Westminster is divided between those who see Mrs Morrell as an evil, conspiratorial figure, 'the lead in Tony Benn's pencil' as one Labour MP called her, and those who regard her as a naïf on a quite exceptional scale. Those, like myself, who tend to this latter view even go so far as to argue that she actually believes some of what Tony Benn says. Others say that being a woman of obvious intelligence, she cannot be as sensationally naïve as that.

She is a large woman, built roughly on the lines of Miss Betty Stove, whom older readers will remember once lost to Virgînia Wade in a Wimbledon final. She used to work in Benn's office with Francis Cripps, the tiny economist, and they were jointly known as Big Frankie and Little Frankie. I was once chatting to her at a party where she was being teased by a chap who was sitting on a tall stool. After a few minutes, Frances realised she was being ragged, and gave the fellow what was meant to be a playful tap on the chest. The crash, as he spun spectacularly to the floor, would have awakened the dead, or at least Fred Mulley.

Those in the Benn camp have, as is not surprising, an obsession with the media. They cling to the belief that if once the broadcasters and journalists would present their message accurately to the people, the working classes would rise as one man to acclaim the policies of Benn. Nothing will ever shake this view. Mrs Morrell reminds me of the old story about the man leaving his psychiatrist's: 'Yippee, I'm not paranoid! They really are all out to get me!'

Mrs Morrell was one of the National Union of Students mafia which fanned out into the British Labour establishment in the Sixties; Blackburn MP Jack Straw is another. Her spouse gave up his job to become a 'househusband' and look after their child Daisy when she went to work for Benn. She takes a lot of her boss's flak; rather as the Queen is presumed never to make an error of judgement, Benn's fans, when asked to explain why their hero has produced some particularly bare-faced misconstruction, will blame his advisers. Oddly enough, she provides some of the emotion behind Bennery. Contrary to public belief, he is no revolving-eyed ranter, but as calm and collected a politician as you could hope to meet. Mrs Morrell, however, is inclined to tears and expressions of utter misery. It is this which makes me believe that she is sincere.

ONE OF THE minor pleasures of working at Westminster in summer is that one occasionally travels home on the same Tube as Enoch Powell. He is almost always dressed the same, in a dark three-piece suit with a homburg hat jammed on his head. Even on the hottest days he wears the same outfit, believing that good Yorkshire woollen cloth works as hard to keep out the heat as the cold. He stands on the platform in a spruce, upright, military manner, and occasionally black Underground guards and train drivers can be seen doing a double take as they glimpse him: 'No, it can't be . . . my God, it is,' you can watch them saying to themselves. None of them ever attacks him or shouts anything. Powell looks so assured, so unaware of his surroundings, so—the only word is 'apart'—that you know before you start that an insult or even a half-brick to the head would be a waste of energy. Like a science-fiction hero, he seems to be surrounded and protected by an invisible force field.

He always claims to get on very well with coloured people, black and Asian. During his time in India he learned one of the sub-continent's principal languages, Urdu. Once on a polling day in Wolverhampton he astonished a group of Asian women by delivering a speech to them in this language. They were the more surprised because it was the wrong one. They were Gujarati speakers, and he might as well have been addressing them in fluent Welsh. I once had the job of taking him to the door in a fancy restaurant in Westminster. (He had begun his meal by saying, 'We shall be talking tripe so I might as well eat it too.') I remembered that the hat check girl in this restaurant was black, and at that very moment he said, 'I am very glad you are accompanying me to the door. You have saved me from a most embarrassing situation.' I thought how awful it was, he was about to harangue the girl, tell her to go home, there was about to be a terrible scene when he smiled and said, 'You see I have no change with me. If you are able to give me ten pence, I shall give it to the girl as a tip.' He was utterly charming as the young woman handed him his hat and coat, and she beamed broadly back at him.

Powell is well aware of the effect he creates and enjoys it mightily. He even mythologises himself. Some time ago

47

I was part of a curious conversation in which someone told a story about George Thomas, who had recently become Speaker of the House. The story was that he had been asked if his mother was not tremendously proud of his becoming Speaker, and Thomas was alleged to have replied, 'No, she was much prouder when I became chairman of the Bank of Wales.' Powell chipped in: 'That story cannot be true, for George's mother died before he became Speaker.' The chap who had told the anecdote grumbled gently: 'There you go, Enoch spoiling a perfectly good tale,' and Powell replied: 'Ah, but I have not spoiled it. For when you next tell the story you will say, "And then *Enoch* said . . ." and it will be a much better story!' Again one felt that strange sense of apartness, as if he had been floating above us, watching the conversation as an outsider even while taking part in it.

WHAT A DELIGHT it always is to run into Syd Bidwell, the Labour MP for Southall, and one of the best friends Britain's immigrant communities have. It has to be said that Syd is not really one of Parliament's intellectuals, but then no legislature, with claims to be truly representative, could be filled with people who are a cross between Einstein, J. K. Galbraith and Fred Housego, winner of 'Mastermind'. Syd once remarked, 'Y'know, that Harold Wilson is a very brilliant man. He often seems to know what I'm saying before I finish the sentence.' ('Or indeed before you start,' someone added, *sotto voce*, at the time.)

On another occasion he was arguing with the then Home Secretary, Merlyn Rees, about a select committee report on immigration. The committee, of which Syd had been a member, had decided in favour of the Conservatives' 'quota' system, by which each country would be allowed a fixed number of immigrants per year. The plan was highly controversial because it might have kept out people who had a legal right to come in; indeed it was so controversial that the Conservatives have since dropped it.

'But Merlyn,' Syd protested at the groaning Home

Secretary, 'surely you don't think that by signing this report I've given succour to the Conservatives?' Mr Rees removed his face from his hands and said slowly: 'Oh Syd, wrong spelling of "sucker".'

What is not in doubt is Mr Bidwell's lack of any racial bias whatsoever and his unremitting work for all his constituents, work which might valuably be emulated by some rather more expensively educated MPs. The other day he was speaking on their behalf in the House and delivered himself of this runic statement: 'I have a lot of second-generation young people in my constituency!' As with so many of Syd's remarks, I *think* I know what he meant.

SLAVISH THATCHER SUPPORTER, Aberdeen MP Albert McQuarrie, has broken ranks to support the claims of Gibraltar citizens to be exempted from the British Nationality Act. He led the protest which created a sizeable, though unsuccessful, rebellion against the Government the other day. Waggish Tories have christened Albert's daring campaign 'Rock Against Thatcher'.

TO THE PORCHESTER HALL in London the other day to attend a monster rally for the Social Democratic Party. The hall was almost packed, with hundreds of people present. Apart from the hecklers they were almost entirely middle-class. The atmosphere was a cross between a wine and cheese party and a rock concert. There were, for example, two wine bars with various appetizing nibbles on offer as well; the idea was, we were told, that we could 'get to know each other better and have a chance to meet Roy Jenkins'. People did indeed stand around with their 60p glasses of nondescript wine (certainly not claret) and hover hopefully near the portly ex-Commissioner, rather like those parties one occasionally attends where A Famous Novelist or A Man Who Appears Quite Often On TV are also present.

When I sat down the chap on my left pulled out a packet of cigarettes and asked, 'Do you mind if I smoke?'—not a particularly surprising request, except that it was the first time it had ever happened to me at a political meeting. When the chairman announced Roy Jenkins, the audience erupted, literally with squeals of delight, slightly above the decibel level I suspect John Hanson gets when he appears in the forty-third revival of *The Desert Song*. The cigarettes man was transported at every mention of the Jenkins name; he would jam his French fag into the corner of his mouth and, his hands thus freed, would break into manic and even dangerous applause.

The opening speech was by Mike Thomas, the MP for Newcastle East. Mr Thomas is not my favourite MP, a fact which will worry him not at all, since his admiration for himself amply compensates for any lack of that quality in others.

He displayed a classic example of politicians' paranoia, when he announced that the press was against the Social Democrats.

'They make a lot of all our hiccups and so on, because they think, wrongly, that sells newspapers.'

Actually most of the papers have been doing their best to speed the Social Democrats on their way, and not because they imagine that politics sell papers. Only Bingo games seem to do that nowadays.

Then Mr Jenkins began. For a man who is witty and allusive in private, he is a surprisingly dull public speaker. The famous lisp is much the same as ever, so that he really does say 'Wawwington' and 'wancour'. He has made a half hearted attempt to cope with this problem by, each time that a word with the letter 'r' in it comes up, barking it very loudly. If you haven't spotted this common factor, the shout comes as a surprise, rather as if Mr Jenkins were being bit in the leg occasionally by a small dog. The content was all right, I suppose, but terribly tedious after a while; one realised that the audience had come for a revivalist rally and were getting instead a mass of qualifications and statistics which left them curiously flattened. Instead of a campaign, they were getting a

White Paper—judicious, thoughtful, packed with supporting evidence and figures, but a little short on the kind of inspiration that would make you tramp through the streets of Warrington these freezing summer evenings. I imagine that the SDP would point out that there are no easy answers. This is true, but there are some pretty easy questions, and it occasionally behoves politicians to ask them.

There were two or three hecklers, one black, all working class and all very persistent. In a Labour meeting they would have been shouted down, at a Tory meeting they would have been thrown out, and with as much violence as the stewards could get away with, but here nobody knew quite what to do except keep quiet and hope they would go away.

Nobody bothered to hide the middle-class nature of the audience when the collection time came. Mr Thomas egged them along by pointing out how well off they all were.

'I know there are a lot of you who will spend hundreds of pounds on a summer holiday . . . come on, I want £20; that's only enough for one and a half dinners in a restaurant . . .' The smoker on my left whipped out a Coutts & Co cheque book and scribbled one for £20 straightaway, and the four or five hundred people present raised more than £1,400.

It would be easy to say that these were middle-class Londoners, writing out cheques which they hoped would save them from the horrors of Benn and salve their liberal consciences at the same time, and to point out that these are the people whom the recession has passed by. But I gather that even bigger sums were raised in the north-east, where the number of people without jobs will soon be greater than the number of people still in work.

TRAVELLING IN A LIFT with a slight acquaintance, or with somebody they do not know at all, most people gaze at the top of their shoes, develop a passionate interest in the lights which indicate the floor numbers, or at most make remarks like 'Call this summer, eh?' and 'Can't see Robson doing any better myself.' A Tory MP tells me that the other day he took a lift in the Commons with Denis Healey. Commons lifts are unlike those in other buildings; usually when you get on at the ground floor of Investment Buildings or C&A, you emerge at a fifth floor which looks much the same, or at least is clearly in some kind of relationship to the floor on which you embarked.

Not so in the Commons, where the lifts must, I swear, travel laterally as well as vertically, wandering like country bus routes around the entire building. You get on outside spacious dining rooms, pass tiny cramped offices on the first floor, emerge groping into the darkness of the Committee Corridor at the second, then cross over to the curious prefabs which have been erected somewhere near the top of the building. The whole journey takes ages; rather longer, in fact, than it takes the express lift to climb the Empire State Building. One feels they ought to mount a small buffet with sandwiches, individual fruit pies, Maxpax, that kind of thing.

Anyway, Denis Healey got into the lift at the top with this Tory MP who reports: 'The moment the doors closed, he began singing, at the top of his voice, the "Ying Tong Song" from the "Goon Show". He sang it till we got to the bottom, and when the doors opened he stopped.' What can this mean? One theory is that it was Denis's bid to get an invitation to the Royal Wedding.

I'M ALWAYS STRUCK by the Home Secretary's ability to command affection, even among people who are completely opposed to his politics and his Government. I recall a Sinn Fein Republican rally in Belfast, held to protest against internment. I was chatting to a woman from the Falls Road who was, at the time, handing out banners and placards marked 'Whitelaw Out' and so forth. We were discussing an article in that morning's *Observer* which said that he was being recalled to London by Ted Heath to become Employment Secretary.

'I'll be sorry to see him go,' she said pleasantly, 'but you must admit that he deserves the rest.' She then went back to handing over 'Whitelaw Out' posters.

He toured Brixton the other day with a pair of burly policemen on either side of his even burlier frame. A floridly dressed black woman kept shouting at him what sounded like harsh abuse. A bystander recognised the woman as a member of her own church, so the following Sunday inquired why she had been yelling at poor Willie. She was aghast. 'I wasn't shouting at him,' she said. 'I was shouting at them police: "Let the poor boy go, he hasn't done anything!" '

I WAS GLAD to observe members of the Government sticking strictly to their own cash limits on spending. Mr John Stanley, the Minister of Housing, could be seen queueing outside Harrods at 8.15 in the morning, waiting for them to open for the first day of the Sale.

AMAZING EVENTS took place at the Labour London Briefing Conference, held to let the lads know how Ken Livingstone and his friends are administering their stewardship of the Great Wen. It soon became clear that many of the more committed comrades consider Mr Livingstone, with his interest in newts and natterjack toads, as a dilettante capitalist. Some of the Labour members present regard the Trotskyists as too right-wing. Being a leftie these days is a bit like being a Moonie; you are involved in a continual fight to prove yourself more ideologically and spiritually pure than the be-nighted person next to you.

There was a meeting to discuss women's rights, and one wretched middle-class male socialist found himself jeered and booed for suggesting that the Labour Party ought to fight for jobs for everyone, not just for women. This heresy caused many of the women present to start swearing at him, and he almost found himself tossed out of the meeting.

The chairman, the former Labour MP Arthur Latham, was accused of sexism because he did, not call more women speakers. He explained that fewer women were asking to speak, and in any case all they had to do was to raise their hands. He was then solemnly told that he should exercise positive discrimination on the grounds that 'women take longer to put their hands up than men because of their physical differences'.

Councillor Valerie Wise, daughter of ultra left-wing ex-Labour MP Audrey Wise, also attacked Ken Livingstone for being too soft. She told the conference that she had transferred all her property into her partner's (this is the modern OK word for 'husband') name so that when the GLC is surcharged for disbursing money it hasn't got and has no right to spend, she will have nothing left to be seized.

All in all, it was a fascinating insight into the way that the hard Labour left will run the whole country when, as may well happen, they take us all over. For example, their response to the horrible rioting which has brought so much distress—especially to the poverty-stricken people who live in the areas where most rioting takes place—was to call for a march in order to protest against the Home Secretary's ban on marches. How encouraging it is to know that the fate of our great capital rests in the hands of such constructive thinkers.

IT'S ABSOLUTELY TRUE, and not a myth got up by the Press: the Social Democrats do spend much of their time drinking good claret. I made a series of meticulous inquiries of Mr Helmut Neumann, the German-born manager of the Firgrove Inn, an elegant hostelry on the outskirts of Warrington, where Mr Jenkins and his party spent the by-election. They had fled there from the only other hotel of any size in the town, which is opposite both a railway station on the main London to Glasgow line and a huge soap factory where the process frequently involves, early in the morning, the passage of huge blasts of air, like a giant belching.

Mr Neumann seemed annoyed at the suggestion that Warrington might be low on claret. He told me that Mr Jenkins had enjoyed, from his lengthy wine-list, a bottle of Ch. Haut Gazin '76 at a reasonable £6.10, a bottle of non-vintage Ch. Bellegrave at £6.40, and a Ch. Haut Marbuzet, not bad at £7.10 for the '77. Mr Jenkins didn't touch the Cos Estournel, which I thought a trifle pricey at £21.50, but one of his guests did buy a Ch. Gruaud Larose '73, listed at £14.10. Mr Neumann tells me, with justifiable pride, 'The claret has been going very well. We have nearly had to restock.'

I GATHER THAT when Tony Benn was admitted to hospital, suffering, as he put it, from 'wonky legs', the doctors discovered that as well as that obscure French illness, *mal de genoux* or whatever it was, he was also suffering from malnutrition. It seems almost unimaginable that a well-to-do politician with a rich wife, and as many opportunities to eat at someone else's expense as a wine merchant has to drink, should have such a complaint. There are MPs at the House who eat three square meals a day, plus innumberable canapés, biscuits and dry roast peanuts, and never once spend a penny of their own. There are whole tribes in the Amazon basin who survive on less than is thrown away from PR functions at the Commons.

But this is less surprising in Mr Benn's case. When he was in the Cabinet, he is thought to be the only Minister in history to survive on an exclusive diet of Department of Energy sandwiches. Very rarely he could be persuaded out to eat in some restaurant, but usually he preferred to take lunch in his office. This would consist of those tiny, wrinkled, institutional sandwiches; quarters of Mother's Pride smeared thinly with meat paste or soggy with inadequately dried lettuce, washed down by mugs of tea. Mr Benn is also an obsessively hard worker, and would never waste time eating properly if it meant an hour away from some cherished speech or position paper. It could be that Michael Foot might try stuffing him with truffles and duck in orange sauce as a last, desperate means of shutting him up.

Benn has always had trouble with his legs. They seem to lead an independent life over which he has no control. A year or so ago he broke one of them in, he said, an accident. At around this time the BBC was making a film profile of Mr Roy Hattersley, the Shadow Home Secretary, who was seen as a Coming Man. They asked him if there was any film of him in Cabinet, and Hattersley remembered that some months before a photographer had arrived to take an official picture of the Cabinet in session. Ministers had heard a peculiar whirring noise and, looking round, had seen that Benn was filming them with his own cine camera, while the photographer snapped away. Hattersley suggested to the BBC that they approached Benn and asked if they could borrow the film for their programme.

So he was astonished a few days later when the BBC told him that Benn had refused to release the reel. 'I met Tony on one of the landings at the Commons, and I asked him why he had done such an ungenerous thing. He told me he was appalled to learn that it had been for *me*: the BBC hadn't told him. Had he known, of course, he would immediately have given them the film . . . I said: "I fully accept your explanation and your apology, Tony." Then I kicked him downstairs.'

A COLLEAGUE OF MINE was investigating the extraordinary affairs of Manchester Labour Party, where the Right wing has expelled the Left from the Party whip in the Council Chamber (Manchester's motto is *Concilio est Labore*, which is roughly Latin for 'The Council is always Labour') and where the Left has managed to prevent no fewer than twenty-one sitting councillors from winning renomination. The Left in Manchester is a very tough bunch and none is tougher than their Leader, Mr Graham Stringer.

Mr Stringer is a very revolutionary fellow. He's the kind of chap who would regard Karl Marx as a right-wing deviationist. He makes Dennis Skinner look like a

Gentleman of the Bedchamber.

Anyway, my colleague phoned Mr Stringer at home in Manchester to inquire about what was going on in that once attractive city. He wasn't in, but his mother was. When she came to the phone, she was sobbing gently. Worried by this pitiful display of grief, my colleague asked what was the matter. 'Oh, nothing at all, I'm very happy (*sniff, sniff*),' she said. 'I've just been watching a film on TV about Prince Charles's life, and (*sniff*) I've been getting in some practice crying for the Wedding.'

I HAVE JUST HEARD another intriguing Harold Macmillan story. It concerns the final months of the Presidency of Jimmy Carter, of whom the former Prime Minister was never a great admirer. Macmillan was asking his old friend Lord Carrington about the last Carter Secretary of State, Edmund Muskie.

'You remember, Harold,' Carrington said, 'he was the fellow who lost his chance of running for President when he cried in public.'

'Why did he do that?' Macmillan inquired.

'Because a newspaper in New Hampshire had accused his wife of being an alcoholic.'

Macmillan pondered a moment and said: 'What an extraordinary reason for breaking down in tears.'

'I don't know,' said Carrington, 'what would you have done if a paper had said that Lady Dorothy was a drunkard?'

'I would have said, "You should have seen her mother",' Macmillan replied.

GHASTLY MOMENT for poor Michael Foot the other day. A Labour Party group had just walked to London from Tolpuddle, home of the famous martyrs, to raise money for Labour Party funds. They were led by Mr Roger Robinson, who is the Party's administration officer.

Foot was waiting at Labour's smart new Walworth Road headquarters to meet the marchers and to

congratulate them on their splendid effort. As he was
hanging about a small boy darted out of the crowd and
grabbed him by the hand. Foot happily shook hands in
return. The boy dashed back to his mother and said in a
loud voice, 'That's really made my day, mum! Just think,
I've shaken hands with . . . Tony Benn!'

NOT MUCH CHANGES in the Tory Party. Just before the
House rose for the recess, Sir Timothy Kitson,
Conservative MP for Richmond, Yorkshire, was speaking
in one of the final debates. As is the tradition, he said that
it would be a disgrace and a scandal if the House did not
debate whichever subject he had on his mind. In fact, he
added, it ought to sit on into the middle of August if
necessary, so that this vital topic was fully and
satisfactorily aired. A number of Labour MPs began to
complain indignantly about this proposal.

'What's the matter with them?' Kitson asked his
neighbour when he sat down. 'Don't they *know* that the
grouse are late this year.?'

Most parliamentary 'wit' is dull, and
depends on the contrast between the
formal pomposity of the proceedings and
the lighthearted remark which is being
made.

THE BIGGEST LAUGH I ever heard in the Chamber came a
couple of days after Joe Haines's allegations that Marcia
Faulkender had written out Harold Wilson's last honours
list on lavender notepaper.

Dennis Skinner, the left-wing Beast of Bolsover, stood
up and said to James Callaghan: 'When my right
honourable friend comes to write his own honours list,

will he take a piece of clean paper, not lavender coloured, and write upon it the following:' . . . at which point two Tories interrupted simultaneously with the single word: 'Skinner!' They were still laughing about that one six months later.

THERE ARE SOME MPs who, however determined they are to create a good impression—indeed, the harder they try—the worse their situation becomes. One such is Mr Anthony Steen, the Conservative MP for Liverpool, Wavertree. Mr Steen has long been the source of much innocent fun, owing to his habit of introducing amazingly far-reaching legislation: his Private Member's Bill entitled Unemployment (Abolition) is still remembered with pleasure. It showed a touching faith in the limitless powers of the British Parliament.

Mr Steen remains unaffected by the gibes of his colleagues. He sees their laughter as proof that there are always those who will wish to mock the attempts of others to create a better world. If Mr Steen introduced a Bill called Crime (Abolition), and you jeered at it, that would simply indicate that you were in favour of allowing crime to flourish.

Mr Steen plugs on regardless with his attempts to rescue us all through parliamentary debate. It is a tradition that MPs may present petitions to the House of Commons just after start of business on a Friday morning. Generally what happens is that the petition is announced, then servants of the House bring forward a huge bundle of papers, all signed by members of the Hemel Hempstead Ban the Juggernaut group, or opponents of capital punishment in Thailand, as well as people with more improbable names like Mickey Mouse and Ronald Reagan.

On the Friday when the Prime Minister began the day's proceedings by solemnly reading out the Reply from Her Majesty The Queen to the Humble Message from the House of Commons on the subject of the Royal Wedding, it was received in suitable awed reverence.

Then, just at the moment when the House was feeling most pleased with itself, most delighted with its role in Britain's ceremonial past, Mr Steen took his legitimate opportunity to present a petition from his constituents. It was from the Liverpool Sex Shops Action Group, and it involved an 'incitement to sodomy'. The moment could not have been worse. Mrs Thatcher looked daggers at the wretched Mr Steen on the Tory benches behind her, and the Government Front Bench collapsed with laughter. What makes one particularly sorry for people like Mr Steen is that they do try so very, very hard.

ANOTHER WEDDING STORY: on the day of the nuptials, David Owen and David Steel decided to swap wives. The exchange was, however, only brief. They handed each other's spouses over at the entrance to St Paul's, and each politician escorted the other's lady down the aisle in a fine display of much-needed solidarity for the new alliance. Some TV cameras unaccountably ignored this gesture.

MORE MPs seem to be facing the end of their marriages. It goes on all the time, a constant parade of small tragedies, hardly important enough to warrant more than a paragraph in the newspapers, devastating to those involved. One Tory I know was thrown out by his wife the day before he was due to leave on a delegation to Europe; she shredded his clothes and he arrived in his hotel with a shirt and a pair of socks he had bought in Marks & Spencer on the way to the airport.

His wife mistakenly thought he was having an affair with a woman MP. Another, I think, was. They were caught by the wife in the back of the family Mini. This incident appeared in the *Daily Mail* a few months later, disguised as, 'He has been seen squiring attractive young MP Miss Y . . .' the first time I have ever seen it called that.

But the great majority of these events are not caused by the fatal charms of lubricious London women, or the pungent aroma of power floating into the nostrils of innocent young girls. It would be absurd to suggest that every single MP is as faithful as the session is long, but on balance I would say that they get up to rather less of that kind of thing that you might expect of that kind of group. The misery is caused by, above all else, loneliness.

A young woman marries her childhood sweetheart; a teacher, or a clerk or a factory worker with a brighter spark to him than most. His work for the Union brings him home late a couple of nights a week; otherwise he is a loyal and well-contented family man. Then his interest in politics wins him the nomination for his local constituency; the election arrives, and within a few weeks the family's life is changed utterly.

Suddenly he is away from home for five days a week. Even when he gets back the constituency makes constant demands; there are meetings to attend, 'surgeries' to hold, fêtes to be opened. His life in London seems far more glamorous than anything his small provincial town has to offer; instead of pints in the pub, there are receptions at the embassies; instead of talking to Jack, the branch secretary, he hobnobs with the Leader of the Party; instead of half a dozen redundancies, he is obliged to consider topics such as the Future Of The Economy, or Britain's Relations With South Africa— Whither? He may become a junior minister, and on top of all the work at Westminster there is an elegant office in Whitehall, a chauffeur-driven Rover, visits to make and delegations to meet. However determined he is to involve his wife and family in this new world, the pressures to drag him away are unrelenting. Each time he imagines he can get home a day early, another three-line Whip is announced. Every time he sees a chance to invite his wife down for a few days, one of the children gets 'flu, or an official visit to the Isle of Mull is arranged.

Many of the marriages that work are the ones where the family have determined to come to London, at whatever inconvenience to the children's schooling and however unhappy they are about missing their friends and relations. An MP who has a home to go back to each night is a better MP, more responsive, more contented, and much less likely to get ideas above his station. I recommend it to them all.

'A GOOD CHIEF WHIP must have a filthy mind,' a Tory MP once told me, and of course he was right. Partly it's because one of his jobs is to tell the party leader which MPs are liable to be picked up by the police in public lavatories, or in West End clubs catering for unusual tastes. Whips also need to hoard pieces of information which may be used, at a later date, to keep MPs in line. This column has frequently pointed out that MPs have much less fun and games than public credulity and their own romantic natures might suggest; nevertheless, whenever they do engage in dalliance, the Whips are generally the first to know.

Of course, they use the information carefully. If an MP strode up and said: 'Look, I can't possibly vote for this appalling bill—my constituents would slay me,' the Chief Whip wouldn't reply: 'If you don't vote for it, I shall tell your wife about that waitress you've been rogering.' It's much more subtle. If an MP has displeased the Whips they may wait for an evening when they know he is out with his mistress. They can then ring the wife and ask earnestly to speak to the reprobate. 'He told us he was going home, and it really is most urgent,' they say. The wife replies, puzzled: 'But he told me he would be at the House all evening . . .' At this stage she might not realise what has been going on, but, when he gets home late that night pleading some frightful engagement and she tells him about the phone call from the Whips, *he* most certainly knows.

These days the powers of the Whips are fewer. It has become mildly fashionable for Members on both sides to ignore party policy, or at least front-bench policy, and a rebellious MP can easily claim to his constituents that he was merely voting for the true spirit of Toryism, or socialism, or whatever. And discovery in some quaint sexual practice, instead of bringing the end to a political career, is as likely to confer heroic status in the pages of *Gay News.*

Recently the Whips have suffered further slights. The splendid junior Energy Minister, Mr Norman Lamont, has taken independence to new lengths. He recently moved from his old house in Kennington, and quite simply neglected to tell the Whips where he had gone. In political terms, this is the equivalent of the number three batsman disappearing to the pub the moment the opening pair begin. Callers to Mr Lamont's old number are told that the new owners have no idea where he has moved.

MR NORMAN TEBBIT, the Thatcherite, union-bashing, Secretary of State for Employment, has devoted much of his political career to fighting the closed shop, having

after SHARAKU

long been a member of the airline pilots' union BALPA which is, of course, a closed shop in all but name. Professional associations are generally much more vindictive than any blue-collar trade union.

I like Mr Tebbit a lot. I think he is very honest and straightforward. A friend tells me about meeting him at the US Embassy party held last year on the night of the Presidential Election. He had asked Mr Tebbit if he was backing the Republican slate. 'Well,' he replied, 'I'm a George Bush man myself. I support the double ticket: Reagan and a heart-attack.'

In September 1981 the Labour Party held its first full election for deputy leader.

CONSTERNATION AT THE Labour Party when the big British publicly-funded firm International Computers Ltd offered to take them, free of charge, into the twentieth century. What ICL said was, in effect, that instead of the usual shambles which attends all voting within the Party, for the purposes of the deputy leadership poll, they would furnish a computer. Everyone with the right to vote, constituency and union delegations and MPs, would have a punched card which they would simply insert into the appropriate slot. The computer would not only give an immediate result, but a few seconds later would print out exactly who had voted for whom. This would save lots of time, argument, and unnecessary effort. Naturally, it was rejected outright. I asked a fairly senior Labour chap, who had expressed misgivings, what he had against the deal. He paused a few moments, then said: 'Well, for a start, no one could fiddle the vote, and then where would we be?'

66

THE PARTY'S ENDLESS capacity for attracting disaster (as with a Thomas Hardy novel, you know before it starts that *every* chapter is going to end in some appalling tragedy for the heroine) was illustrated a little while ago when the now President of France, M. Mitterand, who was then merely Socialist leader, came to address a Labour rally in Leeds. M. Mitterand is, of course, in favour of the Common Market, unlike his British Labour listeners, who weren't.

His speech was in French, and was translated, as it rolled along its rhetorical way, by Miss Jenny Little, the Labour Party international secretary. M. Mitterand declaimed: 'Vous êtes une île, mais nous sommes un continent!' Unfortunately Miss Little misheard and translated: 'You are free, and this must continue.' These apparently anti-Common Market sentiments were greeted with a huge roar of applause by the audience, which rose to its feet. M. Mitterand, nonplussed by the astounding reception accorded his statement of the obvious, continued: 'We must send out a boat to bring us together,' which Miss Little translated correctly. This time it was the audience's turn to look baffled over what possible connection there could be between the two remarks. In such ways is the Brotherhood of Man cemented.

THERE'S ONE THING which is making Tony Benn's supporters furious. By dint of brilliant strategy, they managed to get a leadership election college on the basis of 40 per cent for the trade unions, 30 per cent each for the MPs and the constituency parties. Everyone said at the time what a coup it was, contrived in the teeth of Michael Foot and Denis Healey's opposition. So it's worth pointing out that if the alternative scheme they defeated—one third to each section of the Party—had been operating, Benn would now be Deputy Leader.

AUSTIN MITCHELL, the MP for Grimsby, was cheerily

peddling this line to everyone he met. I liked it. 'I didn't know what was happening,' he said. 'I was just sitting writing my postcards home, saying, "Come on in, the blood's lovely".'

The subsequent Labour Conference was as venomous as ever.

MANY PEOPLE were very sorry to see the defeat of Norman Atkinson, the gentle and agreeable left-wing MP for Tottenham (proof, if it were needed, that few Bennites are bearded loonies who go on heckling courses in Albania). He is no longer Treasurer of the Labour Party and has been replaced by Mr Eric Varley.

It has to be said that Mr Varley will probably be a better treasurer. For, although the post carries a seat on the National Executive and so is voted on for purely political reasons, a certain amount of work with the abacus and accounts book is called for. Norman's skills first came to my attention when he launched a Pound-A-Brick scheme for the Party's new headquarters in Southwark, London. If you subscribed £1, you got your name carved on a brick which then became part of the refurbished building. Unfortunately, it turned out that it cost *more* than £1 to engrave the brick.

A few months ago Norman gave a press conference to demonstrate that the Party was not heading towards bankruptcy. After twenty minutes' desperate wrestling with the figures, he had proved to the hacks' complete satisfaction that the party was headed for catastrophe faster than anyone had previously thought possible.

IN A PARTY which makes such a fuss about ignoring people's origins, Labour people are very keen on boasting about their own kinship. Any miner's son (except Roy Jenkins) can expect a cheer. In the Irish debate, a woman was applauded for saying, 'I had a Catholic mother and a Protestant father,' as if in tribute to her ecumenical foresight.

But the lot of them were beaten hollow by Mr Eric Heffer, who announced in the debate on the police that he had 'relatives living in Toxteth—black relatives'. The delegates were stunned. What could he mean? He repeated it, just in case we'd not heard. Could he mean his in-laws? Hardly, since Doris Heffer has a complexion as pink as Denis Healey's politics.

Perhaps he meant the notorious Black Heffers, whose cattle raids on Knotty Ash terrorised the fourteenth century. Or perhaps they were just miners. In any event, nobody could match this genetic miracle, as baffling as the midwife toad, and if Eric can produce a black nephew—Wilberforce Heffer perhaps—the deputy leadership will be his.

These innocent reminders of the golden years of Socialism, an age when everyone could claim a black Catholic miner for a cousin, contrasted with the vile atmosphere elsewhere at the conference. With luck we may soon be back to the poisonous days of the Fifties.

There was, for instance, the annual *Tribune* Rally on Wednesday night. This is always billed as a festival of left-wing comradeship; in fact the traditional hatred glows in the murk like ectoplasm at a seance. Mr Neil Kinnock was expecting trouble for having abstained and not voted for Benn in the leadership contest. Apart from a few cries of 'Judas', he got off lightly during his speech.

Then Mrs Margaret Beckett, whom some of us recall taking Joan Lestor's job after Miss Lestor had resigned over capitalist spending cuts, rose to speak. It wasn't so much what she said as the way she said it; she didn't mention Mr Kinnock's name and her delivery, shy and slightly halting, reminded one of prize-giving at the Pony Club gymkhana. Mr Kinnock, who sat rigidly staring ahead of him, must have felt like an invalid watching the nursing sister pour strychnine in his drip-feed.

It was all a great pity, since the Rally had given a

comradely welcome to a French Socialist MP. He turned out to be against unilateralism and for the Common Market, but they even overlooked that. He warned, in an accent which hovered between General de Gaulle and Inspector Clouseau, 'You muzz 'ave no doubt zat ever' pozzible means, including zurr mos' nasty ones, will be used against us.' The mos' nasty ones proved to be right on hand.

Many of them were used against the poor Labour MPs, who had their own special enclosure at the Conference, rather like the visiting fans at Chelsea. Normally, in the absence of leadership votes, few MPs trouble to turn up. This time they were nearly all there and with commendable courage booed and yelled at their opponents on the other side of the hall. 'Rubbish, gerroff,' they would shout. One half-expected to see sharpened pennies flying across the hall, and policemen making occasional forays to grab, for example, Mr Tam Dalyell.

One of the worst debates was the one on Ireland. It was opened by a Dubliner called Mr Mike Martin, one of those Irishmen with a voice like a Falls Road funeral, a ghastly blend of rage and self-pity. You couldn't know if he was about to burst into tears or 'Kevin Barry'.

The debate contained every Labour conference cliché. A Mr John Slater from Putney declared: 'I will let you into a secret. There is a war going on in Northern Ireland.' It is an article of faith among some people that the media ignores Ulster, a belief untouched by the fact that it appears in virtually every news bulletin. The general conclusion was that the situation could be solved by the application of Socialism—despite the fact that among the few beliefs shared by both Catholics and Protestants is a deep and abiding mistrust of that political system.

THE SUCCESS OF Mr Alex Kitson, the chirpy Edinburgh milkman, as chairman of the Labour Party Conference has helped to obscure his most spectacular gaffe of a few years ago. Mr Kitson, who is deputy general-secretary of the TGWU, was in Moscow and attended—believe it or don't—a Burns Night Supper, at which he overindulged in the many toasts drunk, no doubt, in Auld Rabbie Pure Grain Vodka, or some other traditional libation consumed at such occasions.

Flushed and pleased with the night's events, he rose to speak and ventured a few remarks designed to indicate his gratitude to his hosts.

'The lot,' he said, 'of the working class in the USSR is much better than the lot of the working class in Britain.'

Naturally this view was immediately transmitted around the world by TASS, the fearless, hard-hitting, independent Russian news agency.

Mr Kitson woke up the next morning with a sore head and no very clear idea of what he had said the previous night. He soon learned.

Meanwhile some three hundred or so hacks and photographers had gathered at Heathrow Airport to greet his return. As they waited, two Miss World contestants from the less well-known countries—Miss Iceland and Miss Guatemala perhaps—arrived, delighted by the splendid turn-out on their behalf, and not a little hurt and surprised to be elbowed roughly out of the way.

Next to turn up was the entire Chinese ping-pong team, arriving for a British tour. They too were thrilled by this evidence of friendship between our two great nations, and equally disconcerted to find themselves brusquely ignored by the assembled populace of Grub Street. Finally Mr Joshua Nkomo appeared. He was on a secret visit to the Foreign Office.

'How did you know I was coming?' he asked in bafflement, as the press of pressmen pushed him aside.

Finally Mr Kitson arrived, surprised, extremely apprehensive, and with a head that felt as if a woodpeckers' convention was taking place inside it.

I HAVE OFTEN written about the way haphazard chance and demented confusion are responsible for so many of the important constitutional and political decisions taken in this country.

The Labour Party Conference was supposed, at some stage, to hold a debate, and a vote, on the question of loyalty oaths for MPs. This would have been a massive and fundamental constitutional change, requiring them to swear fealty to the party and its extraordinary conference decisions.

On the morning in question, one delegate got up and began chuntering on about the need for a vote. To shut him up, chairman Kitson said that it would be taken at 5.30. He then turned off the speaker's mike, and the whole incident was forgotten.

Round about 5 pm most delegates had drifted off to their hotels. At this point one hack suddenly remembered the vote due at 5.30, and asked Mr Peter Shore what was likely to happen. In great alarm Mr Shore asked his special adviser David Cowling, and Mr Cowling asked Mr John Golding, the slight, shabby and highly numerate hatchet-man for the Labour Right. Mr Golding raced up to the platform, counted the trade union delegates with their hundreds of thousands of block votes and calculated in a flash that if the ballot was taken, this monumental change in our political lives could be made by, for instance, the casting vote of the Sagger Makers' & Bottle Knockers' Association. Just in time he was able to persuade Mr Kitson not to call the vote, and in the general confusion of the following day it was forgotten altogether.

Historians never write about such incidents. I often wonder how many of the great events of the last century owe their germination to such trivial incubators.

*In October 1981 Mr Edward Heath
complained that a 'dirty tricks' department
was spreading untruths about him from
Conservative Central Office.*

MR HEATH IS perfectly right to complain about the Dirty
Tricks Department. Except that, instead of there being a
whole department (one imagines a warren of inter-
connecting offices, brisk efficient secretaries, banks of
humming computers, hidden TV monitors tracking
Heath's every movement) there is just one man. Step
forward, as Crossbencher would say, Mr Derek Howe.

Mr Howe is an amiable Yorkshireman whose child has
the distinction of having been educated in Pimlico by the
Princess of Wales. He has worked for the Conservative
Party since time began. Recent posts have included
being factotum to Mr Francis Pym and Mrs Thatcher's
spokesman in the Commons. He is now employed at
Downing Street. Naturally, part of his job includes laying
waste his leader's opponents, and none more efficiently
than E. Heath.

All politicians do this. A fairly innocent example is
getting someone to dig up old speeches which contradict
whatever the opponent is saying now. The opponent then
labels this 'dirty tricks'. When he does exactly the same

73

thing himself, he calls it legitimate political activity.

Some years ago, while Mr Heath was away somewhere, it leaked out that he had been round to Mrs Thatcher's house in Flood Street, Chelsea, to brief her on China. When Heath discovered the leak, he was furious, assuming immediately that he was the victim of a crafty plot designed to make it look as if he had been reconciled to the Leaderene. Little did he know that the innocent source of the leak was one of his closest friends.

The Tories all went to Blackpool in October:

UNUSUALLY FOR A TORY conference, the representatives showed a strong interest in politics. One of them was chatting up an attractive prostitute in the lobby of the hotel. 'You do realise that I'm in trade,' she said. 'Really?' the representative replied earnestly, 'What's it like having John Biffen as your Minister?'

This interest extends to the conference hall, too, making it occasionally a perilous place. During Ted Heath's speech in the economic debate, I was standing near to one of the Tory Party's more distinguished elder statesmen. A young man with ratlike features, dark glasses and lapels festooned with badges, was booing. He turned out to be a steward. 'How dare you, you little fool, how dare you boo a former Prime Minister and leader of this party?' the MP inquired. 'We must have you investigated!'

The same elder statesman stopped a young former Central Office employee who had made a much applauded gibe from the rostrum. 'That was a filthy crack about Ted Heath,' he said, waving his arm. 'Away with you! I hope we never see you in the House of Commons.' At this point I decided to move away myself, fearful that these sinister-looking young men might return with some of their mates.

74

There were certainly plenty of them this year, though whether they are more numerous than usual or just more vocal is not clear. Most people agree that they gave the proceedings an edge of viciousness more often associated with the House of Commons than with Tory conferences.

One MP, a new addition to the wets' ranks, told me that a young man had hissed 'Judas' at him. 'I'm ashamed of people like you,' the MP said. 'You ought to be in the National Front.' 'Oh, no, they're too left-wing for us,' the youth replied. This may well be true, since the Front has a suspicion of big business and capitalism not shared by most Tories.

Like a gardener seeking an ants' nest, I tracked the new right to the habitat by following their path at feeding time. It led to a Monday Club buffet and discussion of race relations. This sounded promising, rather like lambs holding a symposium on mint-sauce.

The meeting was chaired by Mr Harvey Proctor, the MP whose colourful social life has been so frequently reported in the *News of the World*. On my left was a group of young men—mainly in the service industries, one would guess, clerks, shop assistants or prize fighters, perhaps. They cheered loudly at every slighting reference to coloured people. On my right were two sour and elderly Lancashire ladies, who disagreed with repatriation on the grounds that it didn't go far enough. 'If you give them the money to send them home, what's to stop them spending it and coming back for more?' one of them asked.

Mr Proctor speaks in a high-pitched, unmodulated, yet curiously urgent voice, as if afraid that hired agents from Central Office will kidnap him before he can finish his speech. The burden of it was that in spite of the Tory manifesto, immigration was still rising. 'How soon they forget their election pledges!' he said, in a passage which could have been dropped whole into a speech by Tony Benn or one of his supporters.

He was followed by Mr John Carlisle, another new MP. He actually began with a mildly racist joke, of the type you usually only hear whispered in private clubs, or on TV programmes. 'Alien culture . . . alien religions . . . this overcrowded island . . . West Indian parties . . .' amid the cheers someone shouted: 'What about Harvey Proctor's parties?'

Then Mr Carlisle shocked his audience by saying: 'I applaud the British sense of fair play which has brought these itinerant travellers to out shores.' So they hissed him.

Contrary to popular belief, most Tory MPs are not like this, and many of them were angry and bitter last week about the people who booed Ted Heath and who jeered at anyone who suggested that black people might be owed more than a boat-ride home. But these people are not new. They are the same as the ones who booed John Davies, when he talked about Rhodesia in the last important speech of his life. They have been calling for the birch and the rope ever since they were abolished.

Nor are they just the Bennites of the right, though it makes a good crack for the wets and though there are some superficial resemblances. The point about Labour's new left is that they came near to taking power by pulling at the rusty old levers of the party's constitution. The well-oiled Tory machine would be much harder to take into control.

Most MPs have a few extremists in their parties but none of them appears to be under grave threat. The young right-winger who demanded that MPs should be kicked out if they do not back hanging was applauded by Mrs Thatcher but stands little chance of succeeding in this Bennite form of control. Partly it's the Tory habit of subservience to MPs, even when the MPs owe their position to the very people who are being subservient. Partly it's because in the Tory Party, unlike the Labour Party with its ill-attended ward meetings in draughty school halls, the seats of power tend to be occupied by the ample bottoms of prosperous businessmen. For the most part, these people would prefer a safe, solid, reliable MP, even if he is something of a moderate, than the rat-faced chaps with the dark glasses and the badges.

FASHION NOTES FROM the Tory Conference: the delegates are, bit by bit, beginning to look more like those who attend the other conferences. Some girls can be seen in jeans. A man without a tie appeared at the rostrum, though, to be fair, he was booed. Badges are in. 'Wring out a wet today,' one says. 'Who lost twice in '74?' another asks in an attack on Mr Heath. A chap sidled up to me and asked if I knew that the lefty 'Blue Chip' pamphlet called *Changing Gear* had once been titled *The Wet Dream.*

Young men are beginning to affect those sculpted, high-piled hairdoes, once the prerogative of the younger sons of aristocrats, now seen in Berni inns on top of the kind of chap who wears a PVC rally jacket marked 'Team Marlboro'. Ulster's Minister John Patten has one of these—a hairstyle which a sniper's Armalite rifle could not pierce.

The Conference was richly entertaining, largely because it is so unusual to see Tories struggling with each other in public. It's like witnessing a coup d'état in a Buddhist ashram. Some representatives who attended have complained that the press was reporting a quite different conference from the one they attended. They are perfectly correct. The real conference occurred not in the ballroom of the Winter Gardens, but in the corridors of the Imperial Hotel, the first floor of the Town and Country restaurant and, at lunchtime, in Yates's Wine Lodge. This was where the plotting went on.

MY FAVOURITE CONFERENCE speaker, and the winner of the award for Most Ambiguous Words Of Praise, was Sir William van Straubenzee MP, who used to be a junior Minister under Mrs Thatcher. In the education debate, which consisted largely of vituperative attacks on comprehensive education, Sir William paid masterly tribute to 'our brilliant leader, who, as Secretary of State, approved more comprehensive schools than any other Minister, before or since.' This simultaneous appeal to their best and their worst instincts left the delegates sullen and quiet.

The runner-up in this category was the Prime Minister herself. She arrived at the traditional Young Conservative Ball glowing and excited, looking, I thought, a shade like Eva Peron. On the stage she waved an arm towards Mr Cecil Parkinson, her new Chairman of the Tory Party. 'Cecil,' she said, 'makes *brilliant* speeches.' Then, gesturing towards Sir Ian Gilmour, who had made a ferocious attack on her economic policies earlier that very evening, she added: 'And he makes speeches, too.'

Many of the speakers seemed to imagine that there was nothing wrong with the Government's policies; the only problem was the failure to convince the electorate of their unmatched sagacity. One chap cried from the platform: 'We've got to *sell* Great Britain! We've got to sell our policies! We've got to sell Margaret Thatcher!' The far from wet Tory MP standing next to me muttered: 'Agreed, but who on earth would buy her?'

Whatever one's opinion of the Right to Work marchers who came in their thousands to besiege the Winter Gardens during the Leader's speech at the end of the conference, they certainly gave the assembly a chilling touch of the Masque of the Blue Death. Inside the courtiers cheered their Queen; outside, the enraged peasantry came ever closer. Like Death in Poe's story, one or two actually got into the hall, an unnerving reminder of the perils surrounding us.

The mounted police, who protected those within from the tumult outside, were dressed as I have never seen British constables before. Like medieval warriors, they wore thigh length boots and long cloaks which covered the entire hindquarters of their horses, but on their heads they had spherical black helmets with transparent visors, like spacemen, so that the effect was of the lurid cover to some science fiction novella. The most sinister touch of all was that some of the horses wore riot blinkers, tough Perspex shields designed, I suppose, to protect their eyes.

There were hardships for other than the horses, though. Bachelor MP Michael Brown, the member for Brigg & Scunthorpe, complained that, to get electricity in his hotel, he had to put 50p in the meter. 'And it always runs out before I've finished drying my hair,' he said, regretfully.

Over the whole conference lay the glowering figure of E. Heath, a little like the burning image of Hob in *The Quatermass Experiment*. He was actually cheered by the Right to Work marchers, probably the first time this has ever happened to a Conservative.

After the debate on the economy, he was grabbed by Mr Nigel Lawson, the dynamic and truculent new Energy Secretary. In turn, Heath's detectives grabbed Mr Lawson, the Special Branch not being able to distinguish between one type of terrorist and another.

Another curious moment occurred during the debate on unemployment, which was translated for the deaf by a sign-language expert. One speaker warned the Prime Minister to ignore all back-seat drivers. The sign for 'back-seat driver' turned out to involve wiggling an imaginary steering wheel, followed by pointing a finger over the right shoulder. Quite by co-incidence, the chap who was doing the translation found himself pointing directly at E. Heath, two feet behind him on the platform, a graphic and literal interpretation of the speaker's metaphor.

The gang warfare among the SDP's Gang of Four was always near to the surface.

NOTHING COULD HIDE the gleam in Roy Jenkins's eyes, at the press conference to announce the new Social Democratic constitution, when he learned that Shirley Williams had found a new variant on missing the train. She had caught the train all right, but the wrong half of it. It had split before her destination, leaving her stranded in the wastes of the Southern Region.

JENKINS'S OWN political acumen is nowadays not in doubt. He took this column's advice and decided not to hide his love of good living while campaigning in Warrington. The other day he confided to a friend: 'People told me not to drink the claret, but when I got up there, I found that they didn't mind at all.' As Thurber would have said, 'A naïve little constituency, but it was amused by his presumption.'

MANY OF THE SDP people look like young executives who have something to do with vending machines or computers. They certainly love brisk, up-to-date sounding jargon. They're full of talk about ABUs (area bargaining units) and LBUs (local bargaining units) which negotiate with the Liberals.

An ILG is an Informal Liaison Group, and the process is known as 'pacting'. This makes it sound like one of those coy euphemisms for sexual intercourse used on BBC Natural History programmes.

ANOTHER FEATURE of the new party's jargon is that its clichés are actually much larger than the words they replace. Bill Rodgers talked about 'the cash nexus of an acquisitive society'. This means 'greed'.

The first SDP conference travelled by train from Perth, to Bradford and back to London. There was much flexible roistering en route.

BRITAIN'S FIRST NOMADIC, Bedouin conference moved down to London at the end of the week. Dissent and argument immediately broke out. There was cheering

80

and booing. Hecklers shouted from the back of the hall. No wonder the delegates looked hurt and baffled. This wasn't the party of tolerance they had joined all those years ago, the party which had contained legendary figures such as Dick Taverne, Dr Stephen Haseler and Mr David Ginsburg (Lab., Dewsbury). One half-expected to see a stooped old man climb sadly to the rostrum and say: 'It is not I who am leaving the Social Democrats. It is they who are leaving me.'

The trouble was about the SDP's proposal to have at least one-third members of each sex on its various governing bodies. One member was puzzled. If you had one-third men and one-third women, who would the other members be? Volvos, electric blenders and fridge-freezers perhaps. These play a vital part in the lives of most SDP members and yet have never had any democratic representation.

A chap who opposed the scheme was cheered to the echo. Then Miss Sue Slipman, who favoured it, was cheered just as loudly. Miss Slipman is unusual for the SDP in that she is probably the only member to have joined straight from the Communist Party. Would she say: 'The CP is no longer the party of tolerance I remember, the party of Harry Pollitt, Stalin and Beria. It is not I who am leaving the CP etc . . .' She didn't.

This conference has been, almost entirely, a media occasion. Messrs Jenkins, Owen and Rodgers found themselves in a fish-and-chip restaurant in Yorkshire, pursued by three camera crews and several dozen photographers. 'You'd think they'd give them a chance to eat their meal in peace,' one BBC man complained, missing the point in spectacular fashion. Mr Jenkins revealed some of the seamless brilliance which may one day make him Prime Minister. At the very moment the fish and chips were lowered towards his place, he rose gracefully from his chair, so avoiding not only having to eat them but having to appear even in the same viewfinder.

The now notorious and scurrilous sing-songs on the conference train were begun by a few hacks and officials

who, having blocked the aisles, accidentally obliged Dr Owen and his wife to join in. A few moments later the TV crews arrived and began forcibly ejecting the original singers to make way for the cameras, sound and lighting men. One Liberal Party worker was pulled out of his seat by his hair. In such ways does life's distorting mirror constantly reflect itself.

Everybody points out how earnest the SDP is, how worthy and how dull their speeches generally are. But this hardly matters. Most of them are new to politics, and have little taste for the wheeling, dealing and backbiting of the other three parties. They are always anxious to see the other chap's point of view. In Bradford, a woman said she supported the idea of the MPs choosing the party leader.

'If our Leader had bad breath,' she said, 'it could wreck all the negotiations which go on in Parliament, but would you people here at the Conference know it?' A first-rate point, though it could be covered by submitting every MP to an odourometer test and publishing the results. Members would score say, 4-H for halitosis, 7-D for dandruff and 5-G for a silly, annoying giggle.

This tone of down-to-earth practicality, often shading into peevish annoyance that things are not as they were, marked most of the conference. In his Perth speech, Bill Rodgers painted a mighty canvas of Britain's industrial regeneration. But the biggest cheer came when he complained that at present 'If your cooker goes wrong, or your telephone begins to crackle, you have to wait days before anyone comes round'. In the new SDP Britain, one felt, there would be real democracy, an end to divisive two-party politics, and courteous railway porters.

Mr Christopher Brocklebank-Fowler (now known as Chris Fowler under the same semantic rules which attended Mr Benn's march leftward) gave a talk to the Scottish fans about raising money. He made it sound as easy as raising ground elder. 'Raffles always make money . . . get grocers to give you tins of food and auction them off . . . run your own bar, never let a publican get the profit . . . there are those people who think that for them to be at dinner with someone important elevates them to a social position to which they are not entitled. [*Laughter, slightly nervous.*] The fact is that these can be turned into money!'

Indeed, and most of the delegates looked as if making money was an art they had acquired early and efficiently. For in spite of their claims about working people pouring into the party, the SDP is really The Middle Class On The March. This is no cheap smear, either, for the middle classes are perhaps the most effective force in British politics.

They are not like the Liberals, with their faintly wistful interest in health food, pacifism and site value rating. Nor are they like the Tory grass roots who might wish to improve the gas service by birching recalcitrant fitters. They are decent, thoughtful, humane. One senses that some of them were happy to go on voting Labour until the working classes became so, well, so *aggressive.*

Above all they want to get things done. Unencumbered by the ideological baggage of the other three parties, their speeches had a brisk, lets-get-those-sleeves-rolled-up tone associated with the organisation of car rallies or regattas. Nor are they just sheep to be led around by the Gang of Four. By the end of the circus one detected a slight but burgeoning scepticism about the parade of nondescript ex-Labour MPs paraded before their eyes. Asking whether they will succeed is, in a way, irrelevant. They will succeed as Rotary Clubs succeed—because they are there.

*The Liberals had an amazing by-election
victory at Croydon in October 1981.*

WHAT IS WRONG with Mr Bill Pitt, the Liberal victor of Croydon? After reading all the abusive material about him in the newspapers ('If the Alliance can win with Bill

84

Pitt, they can win with anyone'—*Guardian*; 'this political pimple'—*Daily Mail*) I decided to find out. After all, Pitt looks all right; a little too much like the double-bassist in some ghastly modern jazz trio, perhaps, but not frightening to children, like Mr Denis Healey or Mr Michael Brotherton.

'The problem with Bill,' one close chum told me, 'is that beneath this amiable, outgoing exterior, he is what the press say he is—a pompous little windbag. A chap asked me if he was as bad as all that, and I said, "No, he's actually worse." '

This still didn't answer my question, so I asked someone else who knows him.'It's nothing you can put your finger on, but it's the way he says things like "no-one would have thought a week ago that I would become a national personality!" and "Thank you for that warm ovation", when someone claps him. Somehow, one just doesn't say things like that.' Liberal party and SDP workers in Croydon had their own sweepstake on the number of obscure literary references he would pack into each speech. He is well-read, and likes people to know it.

A third man told me that it had been fascinating, on the Friday after Pitt's election, to watch him being transformed from human being into Member of Parliament. 'It's the self-assurance they get from people being nice to them and treating them with unaccustomed respect. After all, if you do fifteen radio and TV interviews in one day, you actually come away with the impression that what you say really matters.' The Jimmy Young programme sent a Mercedes to pick him up that Friday morning. 'Gosh, do all MPs get this treatment?' he asked. 'Only on the day after they are elected,' a Liberal official said drily.

Actually, I feel sure Mr Pitt will be all right. The difficult time, and it is particularly hard for MPs who have won tricky and well-publicised by-elections, comes after a couple of months or so as a backbencher when they come to realise that not only do they have no power at all, but their views are of no consequence whatever. It is a ghastly realisation, and many MPs never recover.

I HEARD ANOTHER intriguing tale from Croydon. Mr Norman Buchan, the well-known Scottish Labour MP, was out canvassing for his party, and came to an ordinary looking suburban house, built possibly in Victorian times. When he climbed the steps he noticed, in some surprise, that the ornamental tiles set next to the doorjamb depicted swastikas—not the old Eastern good luck symbol, but the clockwise version favoured by the Nazis. His suspicions were raised even more when he pressed the doorbell and it played 'Deutschland Uber Alles', all the way through. Mr Buchan's bafflement was total, however, when the door was answered and he, after a quick glance at his canvassing card, said, 'Ah, good afternoon, er . . . Mr Patel.' He quickly decided to say nothing about the fanatic, who, presumably, was the previous owner of the house.

IT'S A CURIOUS fact that all extremist political groups insist on using private code words which reveal their political alignment immediately. The far Left, and particularly Vanessa Redgrave's Workers' Revolutionary Party, have a curious use of the word 'youth'. To us 'youth' means either a young man or the age when one is young. To them it is 'any group of young people of any size, but principally those who are thought to be suffering from Margaret Thatcher, Labour right-wingers or Stalinists'. Thus, 'More than a thousand youth marched for jobs in Birmingham yesterday,' and 'Chipping Sodbury youth sent a raspberry to Sir Keith Joseph this week'. The word appears, like 'media' and 'sheep', to be one which, while looking singular, is actually plural. Miss Redgrave's recent letter to *The Times* spoke of 'hundreds of thousands of . . . youth' and 'Youth can only develop when they learn a skilled trade'. I pass this on so that if you spot this idiosyncratic usage, you will immediately know the writer's political affiliation.

LONDON LABOUR MP Frank Dobson has had a startling

reply to a Commons question. With what was meant to be heavy irony, he tabled a question to the Home Office asking whether, in the event of a nuclear attack, it was proposed to provide places in bunkers for Honourable Members of Parliament. To his astonishment Mr Patrick Mayhew, the Minister of State, wrote back to say that seventeen Ministers, as 'sub-regional commissioners' would indeed be 'located in sub-regional headquarters'. In this case, of course, 'sub-regional' does not mean part of a region, by physically underneath a region.

Who on earth (or under earth) can the Lucky Seventeen be? There are five fewer than serve in the Cabinet, which at least means that Mrs Thatcher can get rid forever of Mr Prior, Mr Pym, Mr Heseltine and other notorious wets, who would be swiftly and irrevocably dried out. If she has any cunning, she will let it be known that tickets to the bunker, like the splendid gold and ivory passes which allow certain Ministers to drive on to the Horse Guards Parade, will be handed out over the next twelve months as a reward for loyalty.

THE HOUSE OF COMMONS runs on opinions rather in the way that some athletes run on anabolic steroids. They provide the keenness, the edge that marks the difference betweeen a competent administrator and a raving, wild-eyed legislator. Suppose, for example, that you were approached by a chap in a pub who said: 'I say old man, what do you think about the National Union of Seamen's Agreement on Sailings of Banana Boats to the Windward Islands?' Naturally you would tell him smartly that you had neither interest in, nor knowledge of, the subject. But no fewer than eighty-two Members of Parliament recently signed a motion on precisely that topic; in other words, almost one in seven MPs felt so strongly that they actually had to make their views publicly known on one union crewing boats carrying one cargo to and from one country.

I found that particular motion in a useful list, printed at the end of each session, of every single Early Day Motion tabled in the previous twelve months. Early Day Motions are almost never discussed; instead they are wraith-like expressions of opinion, undead topics for debate, condemned to exist imprisoned on paper, only to evanesce forever as the dawn of a new session arrives.

There were no fewer than 620 of them in the last session. Between them they attracted more than 30,000 signatures, an endless cloudy cascade of opinion. Leafing through this list is like watching a bag of nutty slack disappear down a coal hole; thick dust obscures everything except the roar of MPs sounding off.

Nothing is too obscure for these boys to have an opinion about it. Twenty-one MPs solemnly signed motion number 182 on painting telephone boxes yellow, only ten fewer than signed 183 on 'Prince Philip and nuclear weapons'. Number 604 concerns 'President Reagan's statement on European nuclear war'. Number 605 is entitled 'Police Dog "Ferdie" '. Number 57 gravely demands 'Respect for the Independence of Poland', while 202 calls attention to the matter of 'The Little Lion Mark On Eggs'.

Many are obviously musket-fire in some arcane Parliamentary war. For example, what had the hapless Tory MP Bill Walker done to have twenty-one of his parliamentary colleagues sign: 'Gaelic Language: Conduct of the Hon Member for Perth and East Perthshire?' Several call attention to the 'Conduct of the Hon Member for North Antrim' who, on inspection, turns out to be the Rev Ian Paisley. But can anyone recall why Mr James Dunn tabled 'Conduct of Lord Avebury?' And does anyone care, apart from the one other person who signed it with him and Lord Avebury himself? Number 323 is called 'Snooker, Smoking and Television' which strikes me as rather an agreeable way of life, though evidently forty-one MPs disagree.

Motion 251 is on the 'World Ice Dance Champions' and presumably congratulates them. So why are there two amendments? Did these wish that the champions would fall through a hole in the ice, or be attacked by itinerant walruses? The year's most comprehensive motion was tabled by Dr David Owen. It reads: 'No Confidence in Government or in Official Opposition.' That seems to cover everybody.

HER FRIENDS AND colleagues are becoming increasingly worried that the Prime Minister is driving herself far too hard. She has always been inclined to work too much, associating it with moral virtue, as befits someone of her Nonconformist upbringing. But just as there are people who drink too much and there are also alcoholics, so she is beginning to over-work dangerously and irrationally.

While she was in Melbourne, attending the Commonwealth Prime Ministers' Conference, she was woken in the middle of the night to be told of some development in the IRA hunger strike. Lord Carrington, by contrast, left instructions that he was not to be woken up for anything. Thus nobody told him that President Sadat had been murdered, and quite right too. There was nothing in that situation which a competent Under-Secretary could not handle. If the Foreign Secretary had been aroused, he would merely have lain in bed fidgeting, and have been in no state to cope with the situation next day.

Churchill left instructions during the War that he was not to be aroused unless the country had been invaded. This doesn't seem to have done our war effort any harm, and it is an example Mrs Thatcher might well copy.

RARELY CAN A politician, unknown two months ago, have become so notorious so fast as Mr Norman Tebbit. His advice to the unemployed to get on their bikes has already summed up and crystallised for many people the apparent heartlessness of many members of this Government. As with Harold Wilson's 'pound in your pocket' remark, you can see what he meant, but it was exceedingly crass for him to say it.

A friend tells me that he knew Norman 'Bites Your Leg' Tebbit many years ago, long before his fame. They were on a delegation to, not surprisingly, Transylvania. (You can imagine the scene in the Hammer film. A coach clatters up outside an old inn, just outside the woods which line the foothills of a black mountain. A clean-cut young man leaps out. 'Ostler, stable these horses! Innkeeper, bring us wine and meat for we are bound to visit Norman Tebbit who dwells in yonder castle!' 'Then you will leave my inn directly and not return, for we do not speak that name, here, in this village.')

The party flew from Bucharest to Sofia, and my friend had a rotten flight. First the stewardess spilled goulash all over his suit. Then, as they came into land, the Employment Secretary-to-be leaned across the paprika-stained suiting and said ghoulishly: 'I used to be a pilot, and this is the bit we all dread the most . . . starting from now!' My friend has never been so pleased to get off a plane before or since.

ONE BONUS OF Ted Heath's recent, and complete, cure is the return of his sense of humour. It's not what you would call a gossamer, elfin-footed sense of humour, and it is often disconcertingly confused with extreme rudeness. Nevertheless, a sense of fun is what it is, and there are rather more chuckles flying around Wilton Street-les-deux-Eglises these days than in Downing Street.

What, an aide asked him, should he tell the press about this huge offer he had received to join a firm providing international intelligence reports? 'Tell them I told them that £50,000 a year was a hopeless underestimate of my

after SHARAKU

worth!' the jovial ex-PM replied. Okay, that's about as funny as a gag by Bob Hope, but at least it is recognisably a joke.

When he made his crack at the Tory conference about 'Don't clap me, it might annoy your neighbour,' even Mrs Thatcher turned to *her* neighbour on the platform, and muttered: 'That's a good one.' She was right too, because the mere fact of using a pleasantry at such a time helped to defuse the appalling tension.

I was delighted to hear about him appearing at a dinner attended by William Rees-Mogg, now a deputy Chairman of the BBC. Heath was proudly wearing a badge marked 'I Was Not Invited To Give The Dimbleby Lecture'.

His sense of fun does have its limits. He didn't enjoy the farce about the Prime Minister's husband, *Anyone For Denis?*, not because it wasn't amusing (it is rather dull), but because he felt it demeaned the office of Prime Minister.

There was a revealing little incident at some frightful motorway service station where he and his staff called for a cuppa on their way north to Blackpool for this year's Tory conference. The staff asked for ordinary teas, with or without sugar. Then the majestic, silvery-haired ex-premier addressed himself grandly to the frightened little girl behind the counter.

'I would like,' he intoned, 'a cup of China tea with a slice of lemon. Do you have a cup of China tea with a slice of lemon?' The girl stuttered that they had Ty-Phoo, if that's what he meant. Then she saw the mighty shoulders heave, and realised that it had been a joke.

He once said sadly to one of his assistants, 'Why do people find me so intimidating?' It's a touching question and it reveals a sad gap in his life, because he can be one of the most charming of men.

MR NEVILLE SANDELSON is the MP for Hayes and Harlington in London, and a lawyer. It was in this capacity that Ealing Labour Party asked him to represent them at the hearings of the Boundary Commission, the body which determines exactly where each constituency should be. The Commission had proposed three parliamentary seats for the borough, one of which would be rock solid safe Labour, the other two having much smaller Conservative majorities. The Ealing people thought it unfair that, while substantially more people in the borough voted Labour than Conservative, they should have only one of the three seats.

So Mr Sandelson accepted the challenge. Unpaid, he spent weeks studying the brief, examining voting patterns street by street, community interests, transport infrastructure, indeed the whole battery of arguments and statistics which the parties use in the (generally vain) hope of changing the Commissioners' minds. In 1980 he argued the case vehemently and at length at the hearings. It was by all accounts, including Mr Sandelson's, a formidable performance.

Months later it bore ripe fruit. Ealing Labour Party learned to its relief and delight that the boundaries had been shifted and that, barring an electoral upset, they will have two of the three seats. Naturally they were immensely grateful to their powerful advocate.

Mr Sandelson was less grateful to himself. For in 1981 he became one of the founder members of the Social Democratic Party, and his work at Ealing could deprive his new party of one, or even two, important seats.

MEMBERS OF PARLIAMENT are not at their happiest during Christmas, for the long festivity bears with it the implication that the country can survive quite happily without legislators. If we can live without them debating the Turkeymeat and Stuffing (European Communities) order or the Sexual Assault (Mistletoe) Bill for three whole weeks, then how much longer could we cope without their ministrations? It is with some relief that they will return from their brief holidays.

(Of course the social style of their Christmases will vary greatly. A colleague of mine had an expensive upbringing. One Christmas Day at three o'clock the butler

93

interrupted the post-prandial torpor by announcing, 'The Queen, sir.' My colleague's father woke up and barked, 'Who invited her?')

Before Christmas MPs have one problem conveniently solved through the House of Commons Gifte Shoppe. This is located a few yards from the Commons terrace and is open all the year round. In December, however, the queues snake round as far as the Strangers' Cafeteria, as members buy their last-minute House of Commons key rings, House of Commons pen sets, House of Commons pewter mugs, House of Commons beer mats, leather jotter pads, book-marks, diaries, ash-trays, a whole detritus of gold-embossed and overpriced rubbish. I can recommend only the superb twelve-year old House of Commons Scotch, and the after-dinner mints, so thick and rich that you could climb Everest on a £2 packet.

THERE ARE SOME frightfully bumptious people in the Liberal Party these days. At the Crosby by-election young David Alton, who won Liverpool Edge Hill for the Libs just before the 1979 General Election, then won it again a month later, was speaking on the same platform as Shirley Williams.

'I do not only look forward to Shirley Williams winning this seat,' the self-important youth averred, 'but I also look forward to working in Government with her!' The complacent assumption that he would be made a member of such a Government caused a rapid intake of breath among the other politicians and the hacks present, one of whom remarked in a stage whisper, 'He's clearly suffering from pre-ministerial tension.'

I HEAR A delightful story from the gallery of the House of Commons where, the other day, Caroline Waldegrave, wife of dashing Education Minister William Waldegrave, was listening anxiously to a speech by her husband—one of the first he has made since his preferment by the Wolverine. As she sat wringing her hands, a pleasant if somewhat nondescript middle-aged woman sitting next to her remarked in kindly fashion: 'You look very nervous, my dear.'

'Oh yes I am,' the delicious Mrs Waldegrave replied, 'you see, that's my husband down there.'

'Ah yes, I do know what it's like,' the elderly lady said. 'You see, my husband was Prime Minister for quite a few years, and I'm afraid you'll find that it gets worse.' She was right, of course. It was Mary Wilson.

SEVERAL DISASTERS attended the recent all-party delegation to Japan. The MPs had the task of meeting various ministers in the Government of Prime Minister Suzuki and persuading them to reduce exports to Europe in general and Britain in particular. Unfortunately, since the trip Mr Suzuki has decided to sack no fewer than fifteen of his twenty Cabinet ministers, which means that the message will now have to be put over once again.

Communications were not helped at all by the MPs' attempts to use the tiny handful of Japanese words they knew. For example, they wanted to say that in the long run a heavy imbalance of trade would be disastrous for Japan. It would be, they kept saying, a 'kamikaze' course of action. Since to the Japanese 'kamikaze' does not imply suicidal fighter pilots, but is a religious term meaning 'wind of heaven', the use of the word in a conversation about video cassette exports was entirely baffling. Fortunately the ministers concerned now have much more leisure in which to contemplate the inscrutable nature of the mysterious West.

WHEN YOU COLLECT Willie-isms, the death-defying logical leaps made by the Home Secretary, there is nothing more horribly frustrating than seeing someone else get into print first with a new and classic addition to the oeuvre. You feel as Vladimir Nabokov might on watching a particularly rare and beautiful butterfly climb into another's formaldehyde bottle. Nevertheless I reprint this gem as a service to those who missed it in other public prints. Willie was talking about the problems of the TV licence fee. Another MP asked whether, in view of the various anomalies, he would examine alternatives. Willie replied with firmness and vigour.

'We are examining alternative anomalies,' he said.

I ASKED A TORY MP about the defection of Dr Alan Budd, who helped to develop the present Government's economic policies and has now admitted that he got it all wrong.

'It is a wise man,' the MP told me, 'who can tell when the bandwagon has turned into a tumbril.'

LABOUR MPS are, for the most part, poorer than Tories, and it is this circumstance which brought about the strange events I will now describe. I am indebted to my colleague Guy Fawkes, author of the Palace of Westminster in-house gossip column, for this short and tragic history.

To save money, Mr Jim Marshall, the MP for Leicester South, often stays with Mr Joe Dean, the Member for Leeds West, in Mr Dean's agreeable flat in Artillery Mansions, Westminster. One night recently Mr Dean got home early and wearily turned into bed. Some time later he became vaguely aware of the front door being unlocked, opened, closed again, followed by the sound of teeth being brushed and a toilet being flushed. He rolled over and went back to sleep.

Again, a short while later, he heard the doorbell ringing. Thinking that Mr Marshall would be able to admit whoever was visiting so late, he returned to sleep, his dreams troubled only by the increasingly insistent sound of the doorbell continuing to ring. Finally he woke up, dragged on a dressing gown and staggered to the door.

But there was no one there. He gazed around, then walked down and back up the corridor, where he finally found Mr Marshall, stark naked, cowering in the lift with his hands cupped uncomfortably round his privates.

It turned out that the hapless legislator had left the bathroom and opened what he thought was his bedroom door (but was in fact the front door), slamming and so locking it behind him. Terrified that other residents might spot him, he had been reduced to lurking in the lift between occasional panic-stricken forays to the bell.

'Why on earth didn't you tell the caretaker?' asked Dean.

'Because he's got Alsatians,' the wretched Marshall replied.

THE HAPPY RETURN of Shirley Williams to the Commons reminds me of a tale which dates from the days when the Labour party lived in Transport House and the new member for Crosby was on its National Executive. She was in the ladies' cloakroom with a woman who worked for the party, and she was staring glumly into the mirror.

'Oh dear, I *wish* there was something I could do with my hair,' she said.

'What you ought to do, Shirley,' her colleague said, 'is to really lash out and go to Vidal Sassoon.'

'But that's exactly where I've just been!' Mrs Williams replied.

EMBARRASSMENT FOR Mr Jock Bruce-Gardyne, the Junior Treasury Minister whose views on monetarism make Sir Keith Joseph sound rational. Mr Bruce-Gardyne, who was promoted in the Wolverine's last re-shuffle, likes to travel around London by bike. This is the cause of some annoyance to the large staff of drivers employed at the Treasury, and it is the Minister's suspicion that they cleverly leave his Red Box, full of vital economic papers, Cabinet secrets, sandwiches etc, wherever they know he will not be—at the Commons if he is at home, at home if he is in Whitehall, and so on.

This means that the drivers then have to be sent to collect the Box, so ensuring continued employment for themselves and reminding Mr Bruce-Gardyne of the folly of his fashionable locomotion.

A short while ago he was cycling into the massive Treasury building when the security man at the main entrance stopped him.

'Just a moment, sunshine,' he said, 'and where do you think you're going?'

'Surely you know who I am,' said Bruce-Gardyne, politely, for he is not a pompous man.

'Ah yes, very sorry, of course I recognise you now,' the custodian beamed. 'You're one of the messengers, aren't you?'

TONY BENN'S re-selection meeting in Bristol was a curious affair. For a start, he was pitted against two paper candidates, both of whom badly wanted Mr Benn to win. The house rules of the new, Bennite left demand that no MP can be re-nominated without opposition, so all over the country artificial candidates are being put up to produce a non-existent contest.

Perhaps one day, just as that Japanese robot which turned on a human worker and crushed him to death this month, one of these humanoids will turn on its maker and defeat him. There was little chance of this happening in Bristol South-West.

The meeting took place in one of the grubbiest Labour committee rooms in the country, and to say that is to indicate a considerable standard of filth. Inside there were faded posters offering lessons in dances which few people perform any longer, such as the cha-cha. Outside there was a monumental mason's.

After his epic triumph in depriving two of his greatest supporters of a nomination they did not want, Mr Benn travelled home by motorway, stopping once at a service station in order to buy a baby's rattle. I wonder why, but I suspect we shall never know.

I HEAR MORE ghastly news about Sir Keith Joseph's

after TOYOKUNI

miseries on television. Earlier I reported his horrible difficulty when being interviewed by Granada TV on the subject of the BL Metro. I now learn that as the film became more and more embarrassing, Sir Keith could be heard muttering—almost to himself—'I am not a *car*! I am not a *car*!' Since the tape was not transmitted, some foolish technician destroyed it, so losing forever another priceless folio from our electronic heritage.

Not long ago Sir Keith toured the ATV studios in Birmingham where he was appearing on a programme. The staff showed him the cameras, the videotape machines, the whole paraphernalia of a modern studio. The Minister indicated great interest. After the tour he turned earnestly to one of the producers.

'Tell me,' he asked, 'do you think that television is here to stay?'

I WAS DELIGHTED to see that Willie Hamilton recently won re-selection in his constituency. Contrary to his public image of a vituperative, embittered old loony, Willie is a gentle, rather shy man, who sacrificed what could have been a fairly successful political and ministerial career because of his views on the monarchy.

He tells me a story which illustrates perfectly the astonishing powers of recuperation possessed by the British aristocracy. Some years ago he and Lord Lambton, the junior Tory Minister who was sacked by Ted Heath after too frequent appearances in the columns of the *News of the World*, were invited to speak at the Cambridge Union. Lambton suggested that they motor up from London in his chauffeur-driven car. Hamilton consequently appeared at the front door of the Lambton town house, was ushered in by the butler, and enjoyed a large, well-aged Scotch whisky in the drawing room while Lambton finished his bath.

As they drove Fenward, Hamilton explained that his father had spent his entire working life in a mine owned by the Lambton family. 'Your house,' he explained in his diffident Geordie accent, 'was bought with my father's blood—your money is really his money. That is why I visited you: to see what wealth my father's toil had brought you,' or words to that effect.

A lesser man, such as you or I, might have stopped the car and ordered Hamilton out. Or he might have fallen into paroxysms of guilt. But Lambton simply made a note, and that year, then at every Christmas for the rest of his life, old Joe Hamilton received a brace of pheasant from the Lambton estates. It is that kind of artful skill which has left Britain with the only flourishing aristocracy in Europe.

Incidentally, few people realise how close Hamilton's ambitions for the Royal Family came to being realised. In 1971 he was a member of the Select Committee on the Civil List, the Civil List being the small fortune (no, the large fortune) Parliament votes each year to the Royal Family.

Hamilton's idea was to put this sum under the control of a separate department of state, called, for example, the Crown Department. There would be a Minister, an MP, who would be answerable to Parliament for the way the List was distributed and spent. In the end the Committee voted against the idea by a majority of just one, and that only after the Queen had sent a message indicating that she opposed the idea. It would, she said, 'destroy the family atmosphere of the Monarchy'. Hamilton grumbled at the time, 'That's like saying, "give us the money and leave us alone".' It seems certain that without the regal message the committee would have accepted the idea and there might now have been a Minister for the Queen. I doubt that it would ever have been Willie Hamilton.

MENTION OF OUR infinitely adaptable aristocracy reminds me of the Marquess of Salisbury, whose family gave their name 90 years ago to the capital of Rhodesia. Soon the city of Salisbury is to return to its old African name. I gather that members of the family, still one of the most powerful in the land, are trying to persuade the old paterfamilias to change his name to the Marquess of

101

Harare—so far without success.

Incidentally, journalists and broadcasters in Zimbabwe are under strict instructions, when writing about meetings held by their President, the Rev. Canaan Banana, never to describe them as 'fruitful talks'. One quite seriously told me, however, that Mr Mugabe had chosen Banana as President, 'because he knows he'll never be part of a split'.

Just before Christmas 1981, it was revealed that a girlfriend of Mr Nicholas Fairbairn, the Solicitor General for Scotland, had tried to hang herself in front of his London house.

WE SALUTE ONE of Westminster's most popular and colourful figures. Step forward Nicholas Fairbairn QC MP, man of law, legislator, wit, bon viveur, self-publicist and central figure in the celebrated Case Of The Suicidal Secretary.

Nicky, as he is known to all his friends and to some of his enemies, styles himself 'Fairbairn of Fordell' in *Who's Who.* He is probably the only member of the House of Commons to have bought his own baronetcy. It comes automatically with the purchase of Fordell Castle, and could be bought by you or me if we had the money, rather as you get free rail tickets with boxes of Persil.

Fairbairn has always had an exciting and chequered love life. In the 1960s he had in Scotland a reputation as a progressive sort of barrister. He decided to intervene in the fracas which occurred at Edinburgh University when the twenty-year-old woman editor of the student paper was denounced by the then Rector, Malcolm Muggeridge, for having suggested that students should be allowed contraceptive pills on request. It was one of those rows where the press coverage vastly outweighs any importance the story might have, and Fairbairn was not to be kept away from such juicy pickings.

Fairbairn, who had backed a local contraceptive clinic, grandiosely offered to take the nervous young lady to lunch at Edinburgh's magnificent Café Royal and told her that he supported her to the hilt.

'Would you like to see my clinic?' he inquired politely. When they reached the deserted premises, Fairbairn sat his guest upon a comfortable sofa and then immediately tried to embrace her. He was sharply repulsed.

It was one of his first big mistakes, for the wronged young lady grew up to be Anna Coote, one of Britain's most celebrated and most militant feminist journalists. She has a less than charitable opinion of her erstwhile host.

It seems unlikely that Fairbairn would much mind. He has always taken an exceedingly robust view of all sexual matters, and of his own competence in this sphere. 'Rape is a crime I have never been forced to commit,' he once told a startled Commons standing committee. In 1979, the dying Labour Government brought in a ferocious Scottish Criminal Justice Bill which, to paraphrase it crudely, more or less gave the authorities the right to lock you up if you had a Scottish accent or a tammy on your head. One clause permitted the police to demand of anyone, at any time, their name and address. Fairbairn attacked this as a gross violation of civil liberties. The Lord Advocate—the senior Scottish law officer—was Sir Ronald King Murray. He expressed the view that there was no time when a law-abiding citizen would object to giving the police his name and address. Fairbairn differed. 'Let us imagine the case of someone who is walking down Leith Street . . .' he began. 'Why should *he* object?' King Murray asked scornfully. 'Because he might have been sleeping with the Lord Advocate's wife,' Fairbairn snapped to an equally startled group of MPs.

None of this libertarian opposition—Fairbairn called the Bill 'a horrific breach in the laws of natural justice'—prevented him from keenly supporting a very similar measure a few months later when the Conservative Government had come to power and he was installed as Solicitor General for Scotland, or deputy to the Lord Advocate.

Given Fairbairn's exotic private life, it is all the more strange that he should have been Number Two to one of the most upright men in British public life. The present Lord Advocate, Lord Mackay, is not only a churchman, but an elder of the Free Presbyterian Church, one of the most strict and moralistic sects in Scotland, which is saying a lot.

Fairbairn himself has an ecclesiastical bent. There is a chapel built into Fordell Castle, and a while ago Fairbairn mused that after leaving politics he might take Holy Orders. One senses that recent events may have put this blameless ambition in jeopardy. It remains, however, a more realistic possibility than that he might now become a judge, the traditional reward for all Solicitors General. The Scottish bench is even more elderly and reactionary than the English. As one legal MP put it: 'Lord C—— would have a heart attack and be rushed to hospital as soon as he read the news. Which would be sad, because he would miss Lord M——'s funeral.'

But Fairbairn's greatest fame stems from his clothes, which look rather as if Dr Who got himself kitted out in Savile Row. He affects tail-coats, silver-topped canes and, whenever he can, the paraphernalia of an old-fashioned lawyer. For instance, when prosecuting, the Solicitor General has the traditional right to wear a full-bottomed wig, so that, appearing in some minor murder case recently, Fairbairn looked as if a sheep had just collapsed on his head. One junior lawyer said: 'I thought I had wandered on to the set of a particularly bad amateur production of "Iolanthe".'

Fairbairn took over his seat in Kinross and West Perth from Sir Alec Douglas-Home, now Lord Home. In 1974 Home was making the obligatory electioneering tour in support of his successor, and was driven from meeting to meeting by a local Tory official. After some days the official plucked up the courage to venture to the former

Prime Minister that Fairbairn was perhaps, well, how could he put it, not quite the figure that they might have expected to take over from such a world statesman, etc, etc. Sir Alec peered straight ahead out of the car windscreen for some time. Then, with a sound like a dry twig snapping, he remarked, 'Yes, I did hear that he campaigned in Crieff wearing lilac gloves.' He then lapsed into silence for the rest of the trip. It seems a fitting epitaph.

HERE IS an Irish story. Every year or so the Irish Government invites a group of political reporters over to Dublin. There they are fed Irish smoked salmon and Irish roast beef, both probably the finest in the world, until their bellies take on the profile of the Mountains of Mourne. They are introduced to politicians, executives, civil servants, popular writers and publicans with whom they then are able to drink until the small—nay, the large—hours of the morning.

The visit has a purpose. Naturally it is quite impossible for a political reporter to be corrupted by anything (as well offer Saint Peter a £20 note and a pair of Barry Manilow tickets to get you through the Pearly Gates), but it does mean that the hacks have the opportunity to see that there are points of view about Ireland which are different from the British, and that there are sane, rational people who do not necessarily think that we are doing a perfect job. The visits are greatly enjoyed and do, I think, genuinely help to foster understanding between the British and the Irish—two races whose superficial similarities serve only to conceal their overwhelming differences.

The last of these trips came at the height of the recent foul weather. The hacks had to be diverted from Dublin to Belfast in order for their plane to land safely, and they were transported by freezing coach to Dublin. A day or so later it was arranged that they should travel north again, by a similarly frigid vehicle, to see the Irish Army in action against the IRA. The notion was to prove that the Irish, far from privily conniving to help the Provisionals, were committing money, men and experience to the fight against them. The Fourth Estate debouched at Dundalk, a small town on the border between North and South were, as I recall, the main hotel used to serve as a kind of officers' mess for the IRA, their equivalent to the occupied French chateau. They were met by Major Murphy, of Intelligence.

He then took them to a display of the Irish Army on anti-IRA manoeuvres. They were, he explained, heavily camouflaged to prevent the cunning terrorists from discerning their whereabouts. Then he took them to the spot, and the massed ranks of the British press were able to observe squadrons of soldiers, dressed entirely in blotchy green and brown battledress, their faces meticulously blacked like Al Jolson, running conspicuously across the glittering snow-white wastes of County Louth.

I SEE THAT once again people are campaigning for more women MPs. I suppose I agree with them in a vague sort of way. I'm just not clear what they hope to achieve. After all, the country is full of under-represented groups: all retired, unemployed and young people are excluded from Parliament, the first two by definition, the last by law. Teachers and lawyers are greatly over-represented, working-class people of all kinds the opposite. White people are over-represented, homosexuals just (only just) the other way. The rich are massively over-represented, as are trade union officials, exhibitionists and men with detachable collars.

I suppose that the people who are pressing for more women (now they even have their own organisation, the 300 Group) think that female MPs will be better on the so-called 'women's issues', which generally means things like crèches, family income supplement and abortion. Yet the women who are at Westminster are as split on all these topics as the men. A group of Labour women, Jo Richardson, Oonagh Macdonald and so on, always lead the fight against each new (anti-) abortion bill. But they are well-matched by the Tory Mrs Jill Knight, whose views on the subject would delight the Pope himself. The campaigners appear to believe that women MPs would be keen on putting money into mothers' pockets where their husbands could not steal it to buy beer, yet it was Mrs Thatcher who opposed a rise in the family income supplement because it would reduce the dignity of the head of the household.

A short while ago I was able, late one night when all good MPs had crept home to their (or other people's) beds, to peep inside the Lady Members' Room. It is a celebrated institution, famous among other things for the occasion when a crusty Tory lady ordered Labour's Helene Hayman out for breast-feeding her new-born baby boy. The child was, the Tory explained, technically a 'stranger' and therefore not allowed in the room; hence the traditional cry: 'I spy little strangers.' I think this incident rather proves the point of 280 more women would not necessarily produce instant enlightenment.

TO GIVE Nicholas Fairbairn credit, he went out in a blaze of glory, rather as the R101 did. People who were there will tell their grandchildren, like powder boys at Mafeking. Already Fairbairn, in his frock coat and with silver-topped stick, has taken on a dated, flickering quality, rather like an old Pathé newsreel. An ambitious man, he now knows that he will never be Lord Advocate of Scotland, Lord Justice-General, perhaps not even be MP for Kinross and West Perthshire in two years' time.

His statement the other day about the Glasgow rape was one of the greatest parliamentary disasters since the Blitz. Each dreadful *faux pas* rolled inexorably out of his mouth, predictable minutes before he said it, impossible to prevent. Anxious to prove that he was no slouch where rape was concerned, he declared: 'I prosecuted a crime of rape in Glasgow last week and obtained a conviction in a case, I may say, in which the evidence was such that one might not have obtained a conviction.' The implication that Fairbairn was somehow exonerated because a possibly innocent man had gone to jail brought gasps of disbelief even from the Commons.

When he added that the crime of rape was difficult, and 'I have had long experience of it . . .' it was too late. Nothing short of a fiery chariot descending from the heavens to scoop him up could, by this time, have saved him.

Indeed it was too late both temporally and metaphorically, for unknown to Fairbairn, as he was speaking the Prime Minister's staff were preparing drafts of his resignation letter. The missive was finished and crisply typed before the wretched Minister even knew that his P45 was on the way. The interview with the Leaderene was brief, and ended with the instruction: 'Sign this.'

It is possible to feel sorry for him. Fairbairn had expected to make a rape statement the previous day. Having been told that he could not make it because his boss, the Lord Advocate, was abroad, he spoke to the Scottish *Daily Record* and the London *Standard* instead. What he hadn't realised was that Heather and her Chief Whip were on the watch for the slightest, faintest

108

deviation from the Code Of The Commons as an excuse to sack him. Speaking to the Press before addressing the House is a trivial offence, and most Ministers get away with it. But then most Ministers don't have exotic private lives and mistresses who try to hang themselves.

When the news about his secretary Pamela Milne leaked out in December, at least two prominent Conservative Ministers went straight to the Chief Whip, Michael Jopling, to demand an immediate sacking. Why Jopling then interceded on Fairbairn's part remains something of a mystery. All Chief Whips require first-rate intelligence systems and filthy minds, yet Jopling did not hear of Fairbairn's escapades until December, more than a month after the hanging incident. Some Tory cynics suggest that Jopling didn't want a sacking because it would have highlighted the importance of the event and thus his own lamentable ignorance.

There are several bizarre aspects of the case which are, on examination, the exact opposite of what the received wisdom at Westminster holds. For example, it was Fairbairn and not Miss Milne who tried to keep the relationship going. A few days before the hanging, he turned up out of the blue and pressed an expensive ring on her. She, a wise and prudent girl, has held onto this.

Nor was Fairbairn 'shopped' by his colleague Michael Mates, the Tory MP for Petersfield, as many Tory MPs believe. In fact, Mates was one of a small group of MPs who decided that someone really ought to slap a meaty hand on Fairbairn's back and ask him to desist. The hand they chose belonged to Sir Michael Havers, the Attorney General, and Mates, who knew him fairly well, went along to see him. Havers agreed to have a discreet word with Fairbairn, and Mates laughably thought he would hear no more of the matter. He didn't go to the Whips (to pursue the school analogy, Whips are the equivalent of prefects, half boy, half master) but Jopling did ask to see him when the news began to seep out. Walls have mouths at Westminster, and when late in December the Opposition Whips knew, there was no chance of keeping the story secret.

Just before Christmas Fleet Street learned about it. The *Daily Star* had it sewn up first, and was preparing to print in its issue of Tuesday December 22nd. But a last-minute phone call from Downing Street, alleging that the story wasn't true, persuaded them to hold it out. The *Daily Express*, which shares a Manchester office with the *Star*, then lifted the story the next day, and on the day before Christmas Eve it was everywhere, like bubonic plague.

ONE OF THE most important groups working in Parliament is the 'Badge Messengers', a corps of men dressed (and they will resent this) rather like wine waiters, and on whose broad shoulders the smooth running of the whole place rests. They are part servant, part policeman, and have a similar role to naval petty officers, which is hardly surprising since that is what nearly all of them were before joining the great stone frigate by the Thames. They are phenomenally efficient, and can track down a missing MP with the speed and ease of a highly trained bloodhound. They also have, like other NCOs, a positively ferocious sense of proper behaviour and dress.

One of their duties is to patrol the Strangers' Gallery, the dizzy height in the Chamber from which members of the public may watch their representatives legislating. Not infrequently MPs who have dined guests in the evening take them along to this Gallery afterwards to watch the rowdy scenes which occur at the end of long debates. It's a bit like buying your nephew lunch at McDonalds and then taking him to see the bear pit at the zoo.

The other day Mr Keith Wickenden, the Tory MP for Dorking, had escorted a few of his guests to the Gallery and had decided to stay with them as the debate progressed. Carried away by the excitement of the action below, he began to behave like his colleagues, slapping his thigh and guffawing loudly, generally acting as if the Boat Race dinner had got mixed up with an outing of Chelsea fans.

The Badge Messenger sprang into action. In moments he was at the noisy MP's side. 'Mr Wickenden,' he said, 'I don't care how you behave in the Chamber, but when you are up in the Gallery you should behave like an honourable gentleman.' I think that is one of the best anti-MP squelchs I've ever heard.

A senior member of the Party tells me that there is now a whole collection of symbolic foods and drinks which, like loaves, fishes and Communion wine, have come to represent the earliest sacred days of the SDP's foundation.

CLARET AND CHIPS are of course well known, and received their almost religious significance at the Crosby by-election. Much more obscure are red wine with cherries and mint-flavoured crisps. These took their sacerdotal value from the Warrington by-election. Members of the SDP were in the habit of going to a pub opposite their headquarters hotel. Some would ask for a bag of crisps and, as it turned out, mint flavour were all that the pub kept in stock (it sounds disgusting, like cheese 'n' onion flavoured chewing-gum). If they asked for a glass of red wine, and many did, it was served with a bottled maraschino cherry.

Already the symbolic potable to commemorate Mr Jenkins's victory in Glasgow Hillhead has emerged. It is a variation on a popular Scottish drink: a cut crystal tumbler containing a superb, 35-year-old Highland single malt whisky, topped up with fizzy lemonade.

MR IAN THOMPSON who lives in Hyndland, Glasgow, sent me a description of a disastrous visit paid by Mr Jenkins to the Rosevale Bar, where he ordered whisky and found himself angrily heckled by the customers.

Some shouted 'traitor', others 'blackleg', and a Mr Morris, of Scotstoun, said, 'You are nothing but a defector from the Labour Party.'

He also encountered a Mrs Grace McGuinness who, perhaps to make up for the churlish behaviour of her compatriots, thoughtfully offered him a drink. 'I thought he was a wine drinker, so I offered to buy him a Lanliq. I told him that it was a famous Glasgow wine,' Mrs McGuinness said. My researches reveal that Lanliq is a famous wine in the sense that Tizer the Appetizer is a famous liqueur. In the bars of Glasgow it is known as 'electric soup'. Connoisseurs tell me that it makes Wincarnis taste like La Mission Haut Brion '61. Mr Jenkins wisely declined. Half a glass could have wrecked the SDP's chances forever.

SOMEONE, SOMEDAY, will prepare a monograph about the role of the Xerox duplicator in modern politics. I don't mean the rather dull McLuhanite truism that it allows documents to be made more readily and more generally available, but the intriguing fact that when people have run off the number of copies they need, they sooner or later forget to pull out the original from under the rubber flap. This means that it can be immediately read by the next person to use the machine. In the Commons, this is a particular danger, since the duplicators are sited around the various buildings where anyone can use them.

Now, it so happens that there is a highly secretive organisation within the Conservative Party known obscurely as 'The 92'. This apparently refers not to the size of its membership, but to a date such as 1892 or, for all I know, 1292. No doubt some event dear to right-wing hearts took place then; a backbench revolt against Simon De Montfort, perhaps.

The ring-leader of this shady grouping is Mrs Thatcher's most ardent amanuensis, George Gardiner, the MP for Reigate. So dangerous is it thought to be an open admirer of the Prime Minister these days that Mr Gardiner will not reveal which MPs (he claims a hundred)

112

belong to his group, though some people churlishly suggest that this is because there actually aren't any at all.

What was not known until recently was the The 92 have a clan within their clan, a body known as the Economic Support Group. It was to these people that Gardiner addressed a letter the other day asking for their presence to give moral and verbal support to the sad and beleaguered Sir Geoffrey Howe at a meeting of the Tory Finance Group. 'PLEASE,' it begged, underlined three times, 'try to be present to make sure that the Chancellor is not submerged under wet pressure.'

If Mr Gardiner, or whoever runs off his photostats, had not left this document under the rubber flap, the world would never even have learned of the existence of this mysterious and arcane group, still less of its intriguing tactics. It was, perhaps, particularly tough luck on Mr Gardiner that the next person to use the duplicator was a research assistant who works for Sir William van Straubenzee. Sir William is not merely an ultra-wet, but the wets' strategic leader, the exact equivalent, on the opposite side of the party, of Mr Gardiner himself. The document and the Group were secret no longer.

YOU CAN'T, THOUGH you might try, help feeling sorry for Sir James Scott-Hopkins, without doubt the unluckiest of all Britain's Euro-MPs. Six weeks ago, Sir James was in line to become the next President of the European Parliament, a job like being a French pop-singer, of no interest whatever to us in Britain but carrying massive prestige and fame on the Continent. Not only did he fail in this task, but the other day he was even stripped of the leadership of the Conservative group. That's like losing the FA Cup Final and being relegated in the same week.

I suspect that the reason for all this humiliation is that Sir James did not suitably nurture the amour-propre of his fellow Tory Euro-members. They have a job of such inconsequentiality that the average ASLEF driver's mate, tucked up safely in bed or in the disco, can feel himself a more productive member of society. It is vital that their leader panders to their sense of self-esteem since it is all they've got. This Sir James failed to do.

He has also suffered from the opposite of serendipity, a series of small but curious mischances. A fortnight ago the Euro-Parliament met in Strasbourg where a film on release was entitled *Sir James n'a pas de pli à ses culottes*, or 'Sir James has no crease in his trousers'. This wasn't a disparaging reference to our own Sir James; merely a strange and faintly sinister coincidence. In his desperate attempt to win the Presidency, he distributed a booklet written in all the EEC's various languages. Like most such effusions, it affected a kind of tooth-grating chumminess, pointing out among other lovable details that he enjoyed playing chess. The French version reported not 'Il apprécie le jeu d'échec', which is the correct translation, but 'Il apprecie les échecs'—he enjoys defeats. Two in a row should keep him happy for some time.

THE BAITING OF MPs is a grand old national sport, and we aficionados are always glad to hear of a particularly successful *corrida*, followed by a graceful kill. News of one such tourney, which took place on the Ealing branch of the District Line, reaches me from a colleague.

He found himself seated next to Mr Ron Leighton, the left-wing Labour MP for Newham who replaced Reg Prentice in 1979. Mr Leighton was sounding off about unemployment in a series of clichés which would not have disgraced the dreary pages of *Socialist Challenge, Militant* or the *Morning Star*: three million, thrown on to the scrapheap, young people in the dustbin of history, Thatcherite economics ripping apart the social fabric. He droned on in this fashion until (I believe) Gloucester Road, when three Underground railway gangers got on to the train. They listened to him for a stop or two, when one of them suddenly interrupted.

'Listen' he said, 'the reason why these f★★★ing kids can't get any f★★★ing jobs, is that they won't f★★★ing work. There's plenty of f★★★ing jobs, if they'd only f★★★ing look for 'em. Any f★★★ing kid of mine didn't gerrout the house and gerra job, I'd kick his f★★★ing head in.'

I doubt whether, however long she tried, Mrs Thatcher could have made the point more graphically. In the event, it was a silent and perhaps more thoughtful Mr Leighton who left the train after this brief encounter with the horny-handed sons of toil he claims to represent.

I HEARD about a clever young diplomat in our German Embassy who will surely go far. He attended a reception in Bonn when James Callaghan, then Prime Minister, was paying an official visit. The young man, who was wearing an exceedingly smart Parisian designed silk tie, was introduced to him. Callaghan peered myopically at the tie. 'What on earth does "YSL" stand for?' he asked. Quick as a flash the youth replied: 'Young Socialist League, Prime Minister.'

ANOTHER COLLEAGUE was able to give me the other day an answer to one of those teasing questions, similar to: 'Does the little light go out when you shut the fridge door?' She was driving home from the House of Commons one dark, murky evening last month. After bowling down the Mall (once memorably described by Alastair Burnet as 'the ceremonial asphalt of Old England') she was turning round the Queen Victoria Memorial when a motorcycle policeman signalled her to stop. There were no tourists standing at the wet palisades of the Palace, no pedestrians along the windy pavements, nor even any other cars in sight. Then out of the gates swept a vast illuminated Daimler with, in the back, smiling and waving to nobody at all, Her Majesty the Queen.

Early in 1982, Mrs Thatcher had another re-shuffle.

POOR SIR GEORGE YOUNG. The appointment of this amiable and capable baronet as Race Relations Minister was greeted with a sour, if predictable, chorus of contempt from the right-wing press, and a series of sad accidents from the more liberal sheets. For instance, the *Guardian* announced the posting in a headline over a story which was about something else altogether.

On the day of the appointment, the South Acton Youth Centre, which is in Sir George's constituency, received a phone call. The Minister would be with them shortly to pose for photographs. When he arrived, the unemployed black youths, whose existence was the whole purpose of the visit, resolutely refused to co-operate.

'You only come down here to get your picture taken,' some shouted. Others, showing positively Thatcherite enterprise, asked simply , 'How much is it worth?'

I WAS DELIGHTED to meet a friend the other day who had been chatting with Mrs Thatcher's husband, Denis. They met at a reception, and Mr Thatcher's description of the perils lurking in his role as Britain's First Spouse was so fascinating I thought I would pass it on to you—as near to verbatim as my friend was able to manage. Denis was talking about his correspondence, of which there is a great deal.

'Trouble is,' he said, 'chaps think I'm in the Government. A chap wrote to me the other day: "Dear Mr Thatcher, seat belts terribly bad idea, don't have anything to do with them." I wrote back in my own fair hand (do I get secretarial help? Do I bloody hell!). Thank him for his very sensible letter. Feel I ought to put in some of my own views, so I say at the end, "Shouldn't worry, Government isn't going to do anything, no chance of legislation." Blow me, wake up next day, read the *Telegraph*, seat belt legislation already passed! Think to myself, "Oops,

Thatcher, you've dropped another whatsit!" Don't know what the lovely lady is going to think about that one!'

*Ian Paisley's Democratic Unionist Party
did spectacularly badly in the by-election
which followed the murder of Rev Robert
Bradford MP.*

IN ALL THE JUBILATION about the humiliation of the Reverend Ian Paisley's candidate in the Belfast by-election, it has somehow gone unnoticed that there were very special circumstances in this particular poll, to whit the events in the Kincora boys' home. Rather unfairly, I gather, the rumours whizzing round the mean streets of Belfast have had more to do with the good Doctor's Democratic Unionist Party than with the old Official Unionist Party. Indeed, the much-reported scuffling outside the count had little to do with politics, and a lot to do with Official Unionists making barbed little jokettes to Democratic Unionists on the lines of: 'Stop molesting me, you fairy,' and so forth. Of the three hundred or so spoiled ballot papers, 279 (I am told) had messages scrawled on them referring to the alleged sexual preferences of DUP supporters.

All of this is richly larded with irony, for the Doctor has for years been in the forefront of the campaign to prevent the legislation, in Northern Ireland, of homosexual behaviour. One MP suggested last week that he would now have to change his battle-cry and slogan from 'Save Ulster From Sodomy' to 'Save Ulster From Even More Sodomy'.

Another militant anti-Papal priest stood against Roy Jenkins in the Hillhead by-election. He is Pastor Jack Glass, and some idea of the strength of his views may be gained from Dr Paisley himself. Mr Frank McElhone, a Glasgow Labour MP, told the Reverend Doctor that he

had visited Hillhead and had met Mr Glass. 'Be careful of that man,' warned Paisley, 'he's an extremist.'

Rab Butler died in March 1982.

HOW SAD TO SEE Rab Butler's death announced, and on Budget day as well. He would not, I believe, have particularly enjoyed Sir Geoffrey's speech. Unlike Howe, who appears to bear somewhat tedious good will to most men, Butler was a master of the extraordinarily offensive remark to which nobody could actually object. A Tory MP tells me that on one occasion he had been lunching next to Butler at the Carlton Club. They had a long and friendly conversation. The MP rose to make his goodbyes, then as he left the dining room he heard someone else ask Butler, 'Who was that?' Butler, using just sufficiently loud a voice to make certain that my friend could hear, said, 'Oh, that's X. He's of no significance.'

For years, before the start of the Tory Party conference, Butler would run through the agenda with the political correspondents. At one point he would say of his Prime Minister: 'And then of course dear Anthony will make the speech he *always* makes so well.' He was perhaps the greatest master of the insult cast in the shape of a compliment.

He was also a superlative Leader of the House. This job requires an ability to keep all one's 634 fellow MPs happy, and is, of course, quite impossible. MPs rant and rage about the disgraceful absence of a debate on child allowances, or the nuclear threat, or the perils facing the paper doily industry. Butler would pause gravely and say, 'I have this matter at the front of my mind,' where of course it remained forever. But nobody could ever complain.

Oddly enough his most famous remark—as I have

pointed out before—was not made by him at all. A reporter asked him if Eden was the best Prime Minister we had, and Butler replied 'Yes'.

He always admitted to not having invented the phrase, though it was really a perfect example of his favourite kind of remark: the one which causes unease because you can't quite work out what it means. For example, of the Press Association reporter who asked him the question, he would always say: 'I have his *name*.' Why? Did he mean he would give it to anyone who inquired? Was it an old man's vague irrelevance? Did he propose to send hired thugs round to the reporter's house? Nobody ever quite knew.

Jo Grimond once invited him to dinner on a Wednesday, and Butler, instead of replying, said cryptically: 'If you had invited me on Tuesday, I could not have come.' The mind, unable to grasp at anything, begins to spin gently out of control when asked to cope with such a remark.

Considering that he could easily have had the premiership in 1963, it is surprising what little regard he had for those Premiers under whom he served. On being told that Eden was the son of a mad baronet and a beautiful woman, he remarked: 'That's the trouble with Anthony—half mad baronet, half beautiful woman.'

I may be mistaken, but amid the hundreds of tributes from statesmen all over the world, one appears to be missing—that of the Rt Hon Harold Macmillan. Perhaps his is so fulsome that it is taking a long time to compose.

TWO INTRIGUING straws in the social wind: a couple I know have been house-hunting in Clapham. A fairly snooty 'negotiator' from the estate agents' was showing them around a house. 'You'll find this a very agreeable area,' she told them. 'It hasn't gone black yet.'

'We don't care about that,' they said, 'but has it gone SDP yet?'

Another friend of mine is a married woman who lives in North London. Some months ago her husband joined the

SDP. She complained to her friends and relatives that he was spending four or five nights a week at party meetings. This seemed to her rather too many, even for a new convert. Then the other day she phoned in some distress. She had just discovered that he was attending, at most, one SDP meeting a week. The other nights he was with another woman.

I believe this to be the first recorded instance of the SDP being used as an excuse and is a significant moment in our history—just like the first man to ring home to say he would be working late at the office.

In Spring 1982, Mr Whitelaw came under ferocious attack for his alleged soft line against criminals, rioters and other people who do not always vote Conservative.

HOW GHASTLY to watch the right-wing yahoos of the Conservative Party in full cry against Mr Whitelaw who, for all his faults, is a decent and humane man who realised a long time ago that there are no simple answers to anything. Not that this bothers the Hell's Bigots of the Tory Party. Mr Ivor Stanbrook, for instance, has been approaching journalists and saying, 'If you want an anti-Whitelaw line, I'm your man.' I should warn Mr Stanbrook that this simply isn't done in the party. It does not become a gentleman, rather like turning up at White's Club with a pack of pornographic playing-cards.

Willie, I gather, has taken all this baying with his customary fortitude and stoicism, shored up by his deep contempt for the Tory Right. The trouble is that they know how much he despises them, so they are moved to re-double the vehemence of their expletives.

The other day he was chatting with one of his junior Ministers, Mr Patrick Mayhew, who told him that under the present law, breaking and entering does not count as a crime unless something has been stolen, a fact now known to Mr Michael Fagan. 'My God,' Willie said, 'do you mean that if I got back to my house and found the window smashed and Ivor Stanbrook in my bed, I could not get him for breaking and entering?'

'Ah, yes, Willie,' replied the calming Mayhew, 'I think that would amount to a breach of the peace.'

QUITE RECENTLY THE Home Secretary found himself at a peculiar function in Oxford. A church there had invited a number of prominent laymen to answer questions from the pulpit.

It was a Church of England church, but a disconcertingly evangelical one. There were various spontaneous cries to the Lord, and Willie found himself next to a man who turned and said, 'I came to this service last week and I was saved. Do you think you will be saved today?' Willie said, 'I don't know!' very firmly.

After the questions were over, they all trooped off to the vestry for more prayers. Everybody had to pray in turn, and the session rapidly turned into a cross between an American TV preacher's hour on the air and an Alcoholics Anonymous meeting. There were throbbing cries of 'Oh Lord, forgive this miserable sinner!' and so on. By the time it was Willie's turn, the wailing and the gnashing of teeth and dentures could be heard from Magdalen Bridge.

Admissions of sin, general culpability and utter wormishness in the sight of the Lord seemed somehow inappropriate in a Home Secretary. So Willie declared in a loud, firm voice: 'For what we are about to receive, may the Lord make us truly thankful', and shut up.

ANOTHER EXAMPLE of his quick thinking came a few years ago at a by-election. He had gone to support a Tory candidate who happened to be fairly right-wing. The Advisory Committee on Penal Reform had just presented

I CAN TELL YOU WITHOUT HESITATION THAT MY ANSWER IS UNCOMPROMISINGLY EQUIVOCAL ....!

its report saying that there was little point in sending people to jail for long periods. The *Daily Mail* and the Tory right were, as usual, in full pursuit.

Willie gave a press conference, and was asked about the report. He replied with his usual waffly speech, but the gist was that he agreed with it.

'That's funny,' said one of the journalists present, 'your candidate here said that it should be screwed up and thrown into the wastepaper basket.'

Willie didn't hesitate an instant.

'That's right,' he said, 'it should be thrown into the wastepaper basket, then taken out again and carefully re-examined.'

Mr Jenkins won the Hillhead by-election in spectacular fashion.

WHEREVER DESTINY now beckons Mr Roy Jenkins, MP, he will have made a lasting contribution to our political life through the medium of hand movements. His are, I think, the most remarkable on the British rostrum today. I used to believe that they were, perhaps, a secret code by which a small coterie of initiates could understand the real message as opposed to the words which issued from his mouth. Then I thought that perhaps it was a kind of sign language for deaf-and-dumb members of the SDP. But that seemed unlikely since often the same signal accompanies an entirely different oral utterance. Finally I decided that they were a kind of formal gloss, a necessary adjunct to correct speech, like Chinese 'tones' or the gender endings in most European languages.

Most of the work is done by the left hand. This is held in a cup shape, and gently twisted, as if plucking a ripe nectarine, when he wishes to emphasise an abstract point, such as 'to seize my imagination'. The fingers are outstretched to underline a point: '*Breaking* the mould of British politics.' The cup is held in front of the face, as if he is about to claw off his own nose, when he wants to make some subtle or erudite point. The karate chop indicates, not surprisingly, anger. A circle of thumb and forefinger emphasises the concept of unity: 'Let us *bring* the country together.' Fingers outstretched, arm des-cribing circular motion, is the next stage of this, as in: 'Let us have an *end* to the old class-based politics.' Finally when the entire left hand makes a grab for, and successfully catches, the middle finger of the right hand, that expresses the entire Jenkins message in one simple gesture: 'Hope . . . strength . . . and moderation!'

MR JENKINS HAS, it seems, got himself elected for what must be the most genteel British constituency outside Edinburgh. I was delighted to learn that the middle classes of Hillhead do not say of their menfolk that they are 'out to work' but 'at business', whether that business is running a large company or heaving coal. One constituent quite seriously said that she could not bring herself to vote Conservative this time, 'even if it puts at risk my passage to heaven'.

124

The Canada Bill threatened at one time to
disrupt all the British Parliament's business.
However, the Canadian provinces managed
at the last moment to reach agreement
with Pierre Trudeau.

THANK GOODNESS that the Canada Bill has now fought its way through the House of Commons. Quite apart from the sheer tedium of the legislation itself, we will now be able to ignore those ghastly procedural narcolepts who have furnished so many of the endless points of order which have attended its passage. One such is the MP for Tiverton, Mr Robin Maxwell-Hyslop, who lost no opportunity to inflict his dreary and pedantic views upon the House. One of his colleagues remarked the other day: 'Robin Maxwell-Hyslop is so boring that you fall asleep halfway through his name.'

ONE CURIOUS, AND generally unreported, phenomenon of British political life these days is the rise of the pressure group. It's not altogether surprising—MPs, to keep themselves informed, have to cope with a mass of information, statistics, projections, trends and surveys which would make the brain congeal even if it all came under one topic, such as unemployment, or Flemish embroidery. Since they have to deal, in theory, with every subject which might crop up in the House, the weight is overpowering.

Things do seem to have come to a new pass, however, as the pressure groups actually take over the work. MPs on the Committee debating the new Criminal Justice Bill have for some time been a trifle peeved by the vast number of amendments tabled by Labour MP Robert Kilroy-Silk, and the similarly verbose volume of words poured out by the same Kilroy-Silk. Many of them wondered not only why he produced so much verbiage, but how he managed to do it. The explanation has just come.

One Labour MP received the other day a fat envelope from NACRO, the National Association for the Care and Resettlement of Offenders, which has been actively interested in the Bill. In between the cyclostyled handouts, he found a perfectly typed speech, even complete with little side remarks, such as 'May I now turn to . . .' and 'If honourable members will bear with me for a moment . . .' The entire package had been sent by mistake, and was really destined for Kilroy-Silk who, without this convenient crib, would have been quite literally lost for words.

ANOTHER CELEBRATED SCOTTISH politician of whom I hear news is George Thomson, the former Labour Minister, European commissioner and now Baron Thomson of Monifieth.

Thomson has now joined the SDP, as has his wife Grace, Lady Thomson. It was she who was responsible for one of the most splendid diplomatic bloopers I have ever heard. She was on the SDP's special train which sped party members, journalists and observers from foreign embassies around the various locations in which the Conference was held. One of the passengers was a distinguished and thoughtful looking chap from the Chinese Embassy.

'Hello!' Lady Thomson said to him expansively, 'can I take you to meet the Gang of Four?'

Lord Carrington resigned over his failure to foresee the Argentine invasion of the Falkland Islands.

IN POLITICS THERE ARE also very few unforced resignations. Those who agree to play the game generally adhere to a rigid and conventional code. The Prime Minister of the day makes it clear privately that resignation is expected, indeed essential. The hapless Minister concerned then writes a grovelling letter including some fictional reason for his departure (ill-health, family difficulties, urgent holiday in Benidorm etc) expressing his deep regret, declaring what an honour and privilege had been visited upon him when he was first called to serve the Prime Minister, and the boundless regard which he continues to hold for him or her.

The PM then replies with equal fulsomeness: the years of unstinting and visionary service performed by the departing Minister, the unending regret felt at his going, the bottomless reserves of affection held by all his colleagues and friends. Often the real reason for his exit is not even mentioned. In this way the proprieties are observed and honour is satisfied.

One Minister who refused to play by these rules was Lord Soames, who was sacked as Leader of the Lords last autumn. His may well have been the shortest political resignation letter on record. It read: 'Dear Margaret, You have asked me to resign. This I hereby do. Yours, Christopher.'

ANOTHER CURIOUS WESTMINSTER convention is the 'hand-out', or prepared text of a political speech. It works like this. Every day (and particularly at weekends) MPs and ministers make speeches all over the country. Since newspapers have limited political staffs, there is no manner in which the *Daily Blast* can actually send a man to Barrow-in-Furness to hear the Minister of Transport give his views on the future of the British moped industry. So the Minister arranges for the main part of his speech to be photocopied or cyclostyled and copies are dished out to the press. This is why, when you read the papers, you can read an assessment by one journalist of speeches which took place simultaneously in Penzance, Glasgow and Ipswich.

Of course, some MPs might take advantage and slip into the real speech important or controversial passages which aren't in the hand-out. No doubt they often do. But until every newspaper has 635 political correspondents, one to cover each MP, there is no way of stopping them.

The system does, however, require a certain degree of trust on both sides, Employed correctly it can benefit politician, journalist and newspaper reader. One person who is happy to use it is Tony Benn.

The other day he spoke in Brent Town Hall, and shortly before his visit sent round the hand-out of what he was going to say. Correspondents would have written their version of it even before he rose to speak.

When he did speak, he began with his usual attack on the hopeless bias of the media. Why, he told his eager listeners, when you come to read accounts of tonight's meeting in tomorrow's newspapers, you will notice that they bear absolutely no resemblance to what you yourselves have heard!

He then proceeded to read not one single word of the hand-out, the version of the speech he himself had arranged to be distributed. It's the neatest example of a self-fulfilling prophecy I can recall.

Benn has also produced the most marvellous new phrase with which to rally the troops. I have often admired his debating technique which, like that fluid you can put in a leaky car radiator, is entirely self-sealing. Whenever a gap appears in his logic, another part of the argument is rushed forward to close it up.

He was recently speaking at a private university seminar, and one of the students asked him what on earth made him believe that the new, ultra-left Labour Party could win the next election.

'It's all a matter,' Benn said, puffing on his pipe, 'of what we call socialist optimism.' Or, presumably, what everyone else calls pessimism.

A COLLEAGUE WAS chatting to Denis Thatcher at a

reception lately, before Mrs Thatcher herself arrived. He noticed that at one point a Special Branch detective sidled up towards him and said: 'The Boss is here, sir.' Denis nodded, poured his gin and tonic into a convenient plant pot, smiled a delightful smile and cried: 'Hello, darling, wonderful!'

DID YOU NOTICE how suddenly, indeed overnight, the entire nation began to refer to 'Argies'? it was as if somewhere there is a store of rude names for every nation in the world which can be brought out and employed the moment we go to war, like petrol ration coupons. Presumably there are similarly dismissive terms for Indonesians, Panamanians, the inhabitants of the Upper Volta, and anyone else against whom we may decide to take up the colours.

I have spent some time wondering how the name came to be so universally disseminated. Did it appear in the *London Gazette* (not another *Time Out*-style listings sheet, but the organ in which official Government and Royal proclamations are made)? 'By the Queen's Most Excellent Majesty, be it heretofore known that henceforth all citizens of the Republic of Argentina, its territories and dependencies, shall be known to Her Majesty's Subjects as "Argies" and by no other name, style or title; And This By Law Is Proclaimed.'

One theory is that the term was first used by the departing Governor Mr Rex Hunt in his television interview after the invasion, and I gather that at least until the invasion it was universally used by the Falklanders. But these facts would not account for the manner in which it passed into the language overnight. Incidentally, many MPs do not speak these days of 'strategy against the enemy'; instead they talk about 'zapping the Argies'.

THE CARLTON CLUB, that splendid, glorified Prefects' Room for Tory MPs, has just celebrated its 150th anniversary. The Club marked the occasion by unveiling a

129

portrait of Mrs Thatcher on the landing over the stairs where, until five years ago, women were not even allowed to set foot. It was feared that if they did, they might be seen from an embarrassing angle by the MPs gathered in 'Cads' Corner', the area under the stairwell. Or so the legend has it.

The ceremony reminded one elderly member of the occasion a few years ago when Harold Macmillan, then President of the Club, unveiled a small head-and-shoulders figure depicting the Leader of the Conservative Party. He tottered towards the effigy in his usual celebrated imitation of an elderly man, then muttered loudly enough for everyone to hear: 'I must remember I am unveiling a bust of Margaret Thatcher—not Margaret Thatcher's bust.'

AS I HAVE REPORTED before, Denis Thatcher loathes and detests the portrayal of himself by John Wells in the play *Anyone for Denis?*. In particular he is offended by the implication that he is a doddering ninny, incapable of organising a drink for himself without having someone hold the bottle. He points out, quite correctly, that he has run many large and demanding business organisations with some success. He adds that the only reason he didn't explode with anger at the time he saw the play was because the function was raising £40,000 for charity.

The trouble is that, unwittingly or not, he does keep acting exactly like Mr Wells's character in the play. Take this (nearly verbatim) expression of his views about rioting, vouchsafed at a reception in Downing Street.

'You get a lot of these golliwogs rioting and throwing stones at the police, and it's all over the television. But as soon as our brilliant police move in and sort them out, there's not a thing about it on television. Do you know why? I'll tell you why. It's because our television people are a lot of pinkoes and closet Marxists. That's why.'

A short while ago Denis and his wife were in Yorkshire, where she had agreed to take part in a TV programme (manned, possibly, by powder blues and closet

DENIS & MARGARET THATCHER

after SHARAKU

Conservatives) about the Great Prime Ministers of History. She was greeted by an actor dressed as William Pitt and was asked to stand in a studio mock-up of Downing Street in Georgian times.

'Hang on a moment,' said Denis. 'Something wrong here. What's that pub doing on the corner?'

'Ah yes, Mr Thatcher,' one of the production team explained, 'it's quite accurate. You see there used to be a pub next to Number Ten in those days.'

Someone who was present tells me that a faraway gleam of pleasure shone in Denis's eyes. 'A pub,' he said, 'next to Number Ten! How perfectly splendid!'

I LIVE NOT ALL THAT far from Roy Jenkins, and the other day I was walking towards the Tube station which is nearest to us both. As I stepped over his street I was forced suddenly back on to the kerb by a smart navy blue Ford Granada 2.8 litre chauffeur-driven limousine. I glanced up in some annoyance and saw that sitting in the back, going through his papers and smoking a cigar as big as Harry Belafonte's forearm, was the new Member of Parliament for Hillhead.

The image was so powerful, so much a part of British political metaphor and iconography, that I felt part of a cartoon, labelled perhaps 'Toiling Masses' or 'Starving Children of Britain's Cities'. Jenkins himself ought to have been wearing a silk hat with a Union Jack on top, like those spindly Russian cartoons in *Krokodil*.

I actually don't mind in the least Mr Jenkins being driven to work. The trip takes 45 minutes by Tube and on foot, so he saves a valuable hour and a half a day. He is also welcome, as far as I am concerned, to smoke two dozen cigars a day and drink a magnum of Mouton-Rothschild with his lunch.

But I should warn him that image is still important to people in Britain. They will not necessarily wish to vote for someone who sweeps past them in a fast car, literally or metaphorically, wreathed in rings of cigar smoke.

MEANWHILE THE FAINTEST, most sibilant stories are travelling around the Palace of Westminster, asserting that Francis Pym, is being, how can they put it, just a trifle more inclined to agreement than Her Ladyship, just a shade more liable to keep an open mind. The Commons is a marvellous ambient medium for rumours, like the Whispering Gallery of St Paul's; however hushed they are as they begin life, they always return later in exactly the form they went out.

Someone in the Smoking Room remarks that they had lunch the other day with X who had just come from a meeting with Francis, and of course he thinks we ought not to get too hung on this issue of Y, or Z. These whispers then reach out through the building, subtly shaping the new Foreign Secretary's image, gently distancing him from any disasters which may loom for us.

Does he begin the whispers himself, deliberately? Perhaps he does, but then perhaps he doesn't need to. He is certainly going to some trouble to win the loyalty of his new colleagues at the Foreign Office. In his first week he held no fewer than three meetings of all his Ministers— more than Lord Carrington would sometimes hold in two months.

TIME NOW TO admire Ian Gow, the Prime Minister's genial and popular Parliamentary Private Secretary, known to all as 'Supergrass'. He is, some humbler MPs allege, hopelessly in love with her, if in an entirely Platonic manner. One to whom I spoke compared his passion to that expressed by the primitive humans in *Quest For Fire*; it is communicated entirely by sniffs and smiles and short articulate grunts.

Every morning he arrives in Number Ten promptly at eight o'clock, ready to pass on his advice, his gleanings from the tattle of the Tea Room, and to perform his little services. Like the servitor of an ageing princess, he will scour the Palace for suitable young men, in this case those to whom she might wish to speak. They will be summoned to the presence, and there, like some sinister maître d'hôtel, standing behind an empty chair and beckoning, will be Gow. Later, as other Members are hurrying to their clubs or their mistresses or else to meals at the Gavroche purchased for them by the manufacturers of poisonous chemicals, Gow is still on the Committee Corridor, his glasses glinting, listening to every word of what is said about his mistress; who is loyal, who is treacherous, who is merely sycophantic.

It is Gow who keeps the Prime Ministerial whisky glass topped up during those testing late-night sessions at Number Ten, though his own preference is, appropriately, for a 'White Lady', a dated yet potent cocktail made from a little Cointreau, a little lemon juice and a lot of gin. He is, if such a thing can be imagined, a sort of professional husband, political helpmeet of the daylight hours.

Now, it is said, Gow wants to reap the reward due to those who serve the Prime Minister well; a position as a Minister in some suitably prestigious department, one which will give a degree of authority and power as well as permitting him to continue to serve. It will be a just reward.

MY ADMIRATION FOR Mr James Prior has always been substantial, and has been lately much augmented. He was perfectly right to accept the job of Northern Ireland Secretary, even though it was meant by Mrs Thatcher to be demeaning. If I have any criticism of his work in those six sad counties it is that he may be searching too earnestly for a solution. The troubles will have lasted for fourteen years this autumn, and now there are too many people who have a vested interest in their continuing. If peace were to be suddenly restored, if it appeared from nowhere like the first soft blanket of undisturbed winter snow, then all those dreary politicians and brutish terrorists would be thrust back into the Stygian obscurity which is their natural and deserved lot. Like long-term prisoners, some Ulster people fear the outside world and liberty, and seek only to make their durance more cosy and secure. That is why they are so avid to dismiss Mr

Prior's eminently sensible plans.

That said, one can only admire the cool and unflappable approach he has adopted when confronted with his latest problem. Many years ago, while he was serving with the Army in India, Prior became involved in a Great Drinking Contest against a fellow-officer, a Lt 'Spotty' Duvell. The match ended with Prior, victorious, throwing up from the verandah of the officers' mess on to the massed ranks below.

This story has now been widely circulated in the memoirs, published last week, of Mr Simon Raven, who was Prior's best friend and 'second' on this occasion. The Northern Irish take an intense interest in their Secretaries of State, and we can be assured that he will be universally known as 'Puker Prior' before this year is much older. So, seeing him sipping modestly at a glass of wine at a party in London the other day, I determined to ask him about Raven's story.

'Well,' he said, beaming broadly, 'I don't remember a thing about it at all. But then, if it's true, you wouldn't expect me to, would you?'

This answer, with its cunning blend of different implications: that the story might be entirely fictitious, that he is not actually exercised about it either way, its casual air of sportsmanship, its overall impression of amused insouciance, struck me as masterful. Like all the finest political remarks, it doesn't tell a lie, it conveys a powerful image and it means absolutely nothing whatsoever. No wonder they are now tipping Puker for Prime Minister. The story, I can confirm, is perfectly true.

ONE OF THE PLEASANTEST aspects of being an MP is the rule of Parliamentary Privilege. This means that nobody can sue you for anything you may say in the Chamber. Naturally you remain bound by Parliament's own rules, so that if you call the Minister For Paper Clips a 'rapscallion' you may be thrown bodily out of the House by a man in knee breeches with a sword strapped to his side.

135

However, if you describe a member of the general public as 'so vile and so bestial in his personal habits that he makes Vlad the Impaler look like Mr Pastry' then there is absolutely nothing whatever he can do except complain.

This arrangement is not quite as unfair as it looks. MPs are supposed to be our representatives, and it is important that they should have some kind of sanctuary where, like protected species of birds, they can say what they please without the fear of being blasted away by highly paid lawyers. There are some organisations which are so wealthy and powerful that, were it not for the rule of privilege, they would never suffer any serious criticism at all. What is even more helpful, the rules also apply to reports of what is said in Parliament, so that newspapers are similarly protected when they quote debates.

Naturally, the people who find this arrangement most irksome are the highly paid lawyers, who look upon privilege as a fox might regard the electric wire fence round a hen house. It infuriates them and occasionally tempts them into being very silly, as the following example will prove.

A short while ago Mr Peter Snape, the Labour MP for West Bromwich East (or possibly East Bromwich West; I don't think it makes much difference) spoke in a debate on the sale of British Rail assets. He made the eminently reasonable point that British Rail catering was a lot better these days than the national mythology has it—certainly much better than it would be if it were taken over by Granada or Trust House Forte.

Mr Snape thereafter pursued the comparison in terms so witheringly unflattering to THF that even though I myself could probably name a hundred people who would agree with them, they aroused great fury in the sensitive breast of Mr G. F. L. Proctor, who is a solicitor and Director of Legal Services for Trust House Forte. Here Mr Proctor made his big mistake. He forgot the golden rule, which is: 'Never ever complain to an MP about something said under the rules of privilege. It only gives him a chance to repeat the remark.'

Mr Proctor wrote angrily to Mr Snape. 'The allegations

of over-pricing, indigestible food and poor quality are defamatory and damaging to this Company and if uttered outside the privilege of the House, would be actionable.' Clearly, he hoped to strike terror of the Law into the heart of the dapper legislator.

But Mr Snape is not easily cowed. His reply hurtled back: 'I acknowledge receipt of your silly and pompous letter,' he wrote, going on to remark that THF would be better employed in 'improving the deplorable standards set by your motorway outlets. The receipt of your writ will allow my comments to reach a much wider audience; I look forward to its arrival. I must presume that you have written in similar vein to Egon Ronay; he was much ruder than I.'

Clearly Mr Proctor hoped to prevent Mr Snape's thoughtful criticisms from reaching the great motoring public. He would appear to have failed, wouldn't he?

Incidentally, Snape has been telling me the extraordinary story of the Buffer Stop Bar at Euston Station. This has been closed since September because Travellers Fare (a wholly-owned subsidiary of British Rail) and the British Rail Properties Board—another wholly-owned subsidiary of British Rail—cannot agree on the rent which Travellers Fare ought to pay the BRPB, even though both of them sit together on the British Rail Board. Got all that? 'The trouble is,' Snape tells me ruefully, 'they can't organise a piss-up *or* a brewery.'

MPs GET PLENTY OF letters about law and order these days, many of them from places like Brixton and Liverpool, often making the point that it is all very well for Parliament to waffle on, but it isn't MPs who have to suffer the violence on our streets. One such heart-rending missive reached a Scottish Labour MP the other day. The writer and his wife, the letter said, along with most of their friends, thought the police deserved full backing in their call for capital punishment to be re-introduced. They continued: 'A great many people from all walks of life and every political view often express the opinion that it is not so often the likes of Members of Parliament who are murdered; it is more often the likes of *us.*' The letter was signed by the Earl and Countess of Balfour.

I LOVE ATTLEE STORIES, which always turn on the man's extraordinary dry and laconic manner. This is in nostalgic vogue at present, when politicians appear to have far too much to say and far too many different ways of saying it.

Attlee was attending a meeting of the Parliamentary Labour Party shortly after the War, when Harold Davies MP made a powerful and passionate speech on the then relatively new topic of the atomic bomb. It was a towering, even a magnificent speech, and when it was ended the MPs roared their approval. Attlee waited for the clapping to subside, then said, 'Yes, Harold, that is something we'll have to watch. Next business.'

THAT STORY COMES from the new volume of memoirs by John Parker, the longest serving member and so the current Father of the House. He tells another, this time about Churchill's declining years. After his second stroke the old man hobbled slowly and painfully into the Chamber supported by two stout sticks. One young Tory said to another, 'The old man's getting very ga-ga nowadays.' He turned to them and growled: 'He is also very hard of hearing.'

A FRESH QUOTE from my great friend Eric Heffer, who a week ago gave us 'We were unanimous—in fact we were all unanimous.' After a meeting of the Labour Party's Organisation sub-committee he announced, 'The bubble has been relatively burst.'

I NEVER CEASE TO BE astonished at the manner in which MPs like to have everything all ways. Take Mr Keith Best,

138

stocky ex-paratrooper and Tory MP for Anglesey. He was one of the courageous group of rebels who, after the Budget, refused to stomach the Government's decision not to give back to the unemployed the five per cent they had had taken away.

After the debate, Best appeared on a radio programme and announced that, while he had voted once with the Government because he was a Parliamentary Private Secretary, he would refuse to do so again unless Ministers changed their minds. Under no circumstances would they have his support a second time on this vitally important issue.

And indeed when the matter was debated again, and the Government revealed that it had not changed its mind, Mr Best was among the rebels who staunchly refused to do the Whips' bidding and followed instead their own consciences.

Or was he? For among the very first people to rush up to Mr Michael Jopling, the Government Chief Whip, to explain that he hadn't *really* abstained, but had been accidentally trapped unawares in another radio studio, was the diminutive Mr Best. With an ability to please all sides as readily as that, I predict he will go far.

WHAT A SPLENDID BBC political correspondent John Cole is proving to be! An experienced commentator on the whole Westminster scene, he has an unrivalled shit detector which enables him to decide with near certainty the many occasions when MPs are fibbing. However, his powerful Ulster accent can on occasion by a problem.

The other day Mr Michael Mates, the well-known Tory 'wet', found himself at a reception at the Westminster area which was also attended by the Prime Minister and, of course, her burly Special Branch security guards.

Suddenly Mates found the guards clustered round him. There was a phone call for him and the caller had an Irish voice. It was quite likely, they implied, that he was an IRA terrorist who had tracked Mrs Thatcher down and was trying to confirm her presence before launching a SAM missile attack. They insisted on accompanying the now timorous legislator to the phone and listening in to every word on an extension. The mystery terrorist turned out, of course, to be John Cole with a routine political inquiry.

ONE MAN WHO has every reason to curse the Argentine invasion and Lord Carrington's resignation is Mr Tom King, the elegant, persuasive Local Government Minister who by rights ought to be in the Cabinet by now. Indeed he has been promised as much in the past by the Prime Minister herself.

So when Mr Pym was promoted to the Foreign Office and Mr Biffen became Leader of the House, there was a perfect seat for him, all ready and toasty-warm, at the Department of Trade. Mrs Thatcher had decided to give it to him when, on the Monday night of the Carrington resignation, along swept a delegation consisting of Baroness Young, the leader of the Lords, and 'Bertie' Denham, gregarious, fun-loving novelist and Lords Chief Whip. They insisted (quite fallaciously, as it happens) that Tory Cabinets always have three peers in them, and that for this reason she must appoint a Lord. And in any case, since peers who are not Ministers get very little money, she had to keep open the prospect of promotion instead. So the job went to the unknown Lord Cockfield, quite the most obscure Cabinet Minister since the last war. He has, I believe, connections in the retail trade.

Following the *Sun*'s disgusting decision to sponsor a Sidewinder missile with the legend 'Up Yours, Galtieri' on the hull, a small group of MPs and I were pondering what message other newspapers might inscribe on their own Sea Hawks or Exocets. A Spanish-speaking MP tells me that a literal translation of 'Up Yours' would make *La Prensa* of Buenos Aires write 'Arriba el suyo, Thatcher', but this would be franglais, or least spanglish. The equivalent phrase in real Spanish is 'A tomar por culo, Thatcher'. The *Times* chap on the *Invincible* would write politely, 'Sir, may I crave the courtesy of your cruiser?' One envisages the *Guardian* man on *Hermes* writing,

'Hoping this will enable you to see all points of view in this complex and distressing matter, Galtieri.' The folksy *Daily Mirror* would say: 'Hope this finds you as it leaves us, The Old Codgers' and the *Financial Times* would write: 'May your corned beef futures hit the floor.'

The *Daily Telegraph* missile, possibly an old shell from the Battle of Jutland, would be signed by Lt Col Bagwash, DSO (Rtd) and would say: 'All this brouhaha takes me back to my days with the Thirty-Fourth in Penang when (continued on next missile).'

THE FALKLANDS CRISIS produced some perplexing paradoxes. For instance, the attacks on the BBC's coverage came in fairly equal measure from far-out Thatcher loyalists and, on the extreme left of the Labour Party, from Mr Benn. So far the Prime Minister has not been driven to the extremities of rage displayed by her predecessor Sir Anthony Eden at the time of Suez. What annoyed Eden in particular was the fact that the World Service, in its regular review of the British press, continued to inform everyone—dagoes, spicks, wops and damn Yankees alike—that several papers opposed the whole exercise.

The Government set up a Black Propaganda unit in Cyprus which used BBC wavelengths to broadcast to the Middle East, colourfully threatening the revenge of Allah upon the Egyptians. Ministers even despatched a Foreign Office overseer to Bush House, the home of the World Service, to examine the scripts before they were broadcast. Unhappily for Eden the fellow arrived only a day before the humiliating cease-fire and so did not even have time to take his blue pencil out of its box.

Finally Eden put in train the dismissal of the entire Board of Governors, a step which the Prime Minister is always entitled to take, but which would in effect amount to a Government take-over of the BBC. He was dissuaded by more level-headed colleagues.

Now here is the curious irony. The last time that a Minister tried to have the Governors sacked was back in the mid-Sixties when pirate radio stations were broadcasting from all around our coast. It is not generally known that the then Postmaster-General decided that the BBC ought to counter this assault by means of a pop channel of its own—which would take advertising. The Governors, who uniformly (and rightly) fear the lasting implications of taking a single advert, refused. So the Minister drew up an Instrument to dismiss them. The plan actually got as far as a Cabinet Committee where, with the help of the Clerk to the Privy Council, the whole stupid enterprise was killed.

The Postmaster-General in question was Mr Anthony Wedgwood Benn.

WHEN THE FINAL account of the Falklands affair comes to be written, it is unlikely that historians will do full justice to the role played by Sir Bernard Braine MP. Sir Bernard, with his large, quivering, perpetually indignant frame, is a source of much innocent amusement to members on both sides of the House. Yet it was his towering anger which—almost single handedly—prevented the Government from accepting the original 'leaseback' plan quietly agreed months ago with the Argentines. It is quite probably true to say that, for better or for worse, none of this would have happened if Sir Bernard had fallen under a bus (or more appropriately, a hansom carriage) during the 1979 election.

Last week he listened with mounting fury to Michael Foot's call for the matter to be left in the hands of the United Nations. Literally shaking with rage, he got up time and again to interrupt the silvery-haired old peacemonger. Each time he rose, Braine was a degree or two more red; curious popping and spluttering noises emerged from his various facial orifices; those close to him feared that, like an over-extended steam engine or an incandescent star, he might implode, with catastrophic effect.

Finally Foot sat down and Braine rose again, apparently under the impression that the Opposition leader had given way. But this was not the case, and instead the Speaker had called Dr David Owen. For a moment Braine was reduced to what, in his case, passes for silence. Then he shouted out: 'You did not dare to let me say what I have to say!' Dr Owen smoothly continued, and the Tory MP behind Braine leaned languidly back to a colleague and remarked: 'That is the best example of coitus interruptus I have ever seen.'

The other day, a friend tells me, Sir Bernard was taking dinner with some other MPs.

'I've done my bit for the Falkland Islanders,' he announced to a thoughtful silence from his colleagues. 'Now,' Sir Bernard continued, 'I am going to take up the case of the Poles.'

'World War III can only be weeks away,' my friend groaned as he recounted this story.

THERE ARE TIMES when only another Old Etonian can prevent a former schoolfellow from making a ghastly social bish. Last week the Prime Minister had an appallingly tiring day. She gave lunch to Mr Mugabe, her more moderate opposite number from Zimbabwe, and then a massive formal dinner in the evening for Mr Muldoon, the Premier of New Zealand.

As this meal approached its end, and official turned up at her elbow to say that the Secretary-general of the United Nations had come on the phone to say that the peace talks with Argentina had irrevocably broken down. Mrs Thatcher is not a lover of long after-dinner stories over port and cigars, and she was immediately twitching, desperate to get back to work. Mr Muldoon, weary and jet-lagged, was just as keen to go to bed.

Unhappily for both of them, among the other guests were the Duke and Duchess of Kent. There is a firm rule that Prime Ministers cannot simply scarper while Royalty is present, and Royalty showed no sign of wanting to leave. The situation was getting insupportable. It seemed as if Britain's entire war effort could be destroyed because of ancient courtly etiquette.

144

Finally someone had a clever idea. Charles Douglas-Home, the editor of *The Times*, had been a pupil at Eton at the same time as the Duke. He was alerted to the situation, and smoothly made his way round to the ducal shoulder. 'I think you had better go,' he said, and off they went. The relief of the Falklands continued.

The visit of President Reagan was news-worthy less for what he said than for what he didn't.

THERE ISN'T AN MP at Westminster who isn't fantastically jealous of President Reagan's amazing tele-prompter, the gizmo that enabled him to deliver 35 minutes of uninterrupted, bland cliché without once referring to notes. Every politician would adore to deliver a dazzlingly witty speech seemingly impromptu.

The actual device Reagan used is simple in its concept and exceedingly complicated in practice. The President stands behind a pair of two-way mirrors which, from the audience's point of view, look like transparent glass. The speech is projected on to the silvered side where it can be easily read. It took no less than four days to fix this device up, and at the last moment a technician had to be flown in from Paris to make sure that it did not fail and leave the President silent and open-mouthed, as if taking one of his famous naps.

Lyndon Johnson used a similar gadget of an earlier and cruder type when making a key speech to Congress. Sadly, the screen angled towards the Democrat side of the House went blank and he had to address his entire speech as if to the Republican enemy.

I WAS DELIGHTED to see how White House correspondents operate. They tend to be, how can I put it, just a shade less deferential to those set above them than their equivalents in Britain. I only wish we had their nerve.

As President Reagan, Al Haig and Mrs Thatcher stepped out on to the pavement after lunch at Number Ten (a little tipsy, no doubt, from the fabulously expensive 1961 Burgundy they had been drinking) they were greeted by the crowd in general and by Mr Sam Donaldson of ABC News in particular. Mr Donaldson has a quite remarkably loud voice and can probably contact his office in New York without the use of a telephone. As the polite farewell courtesies were being muttered, Donaldson boomed: 'Mr President, Mrs Jeane Kirkpatrick has described US foreign policy as "inept"—are you going to sack her?' Reagan and the rest of the party treated his remark with what Lord George-Brown used to call 'a complete ignoral'.

'OK, Mr President, since you don't disown Mrs Kirkpatrick, do *you* resign?' Mr Donaldson demanded, at the top of his voice. Reagan continued to smile amiably.

'Oh Mr Haig, do you agree with Mrs Kirkpatrick?' Donaldson inquired, then, lapsing into coo-ee speak as if addressing a fractious infant. 'Mr Secretary of State, Al Haig, I'm still here!' The handshaking and muttered pleasantries continued uninterrupted. Finally Mr Donaldson produced a stentorian shout, as if warning the Thurber family of the imminent destruction of the Columbus, Ohio, dam, and yelled: 'OK, is there anyone on that sidewalk over there who does not believe that our foreign policy is inept?'

At this point Mr Haig cracked, and glowering at Mr Donaldson raised his fingers in a reverse V, or Victory, sign. I do not know what he can have meant by this.

At the press conference which followed, one of the American reporters was even more blunt. 'Why don'tcha sack the silly old bitch?' he asked. I admire this approach, and feel it should be extended to Britain. For starters, correspondents should be allowed to shout imprecations from the Press Gallery into the Chamber. They would, I'd wager, be rather wittier and crisper than the ones presently shouted downstairs.

THERE IS A POPULAR and grisly form of blood sport engaged in by MPs. It generally takes place on a Friday afternoon at the end of business. It is the (almost) weekly massacre of Private Members' Bills, a sort of permanent year-round, Glorious Twelfth.

Most Private Members' Bills are debated either skimpily or not at all. A tiny minority are so bland and anodyne that they become law or at any rate get a second reading, without any discussion.

The rest, however, have their titles read out by the Clerks, and, if a single member shouts the word 'Object!' they fail to get a second reading, and go to the back of the queue. This queue, like people waiting for second helpings in a workhouse, or the sad straggling line outside the US Visa Office in Mexico City, is virtually endless. Even to reach the head of it does not guarantee, or even suggest, that you will get what you came for.

The most famous of all 'Objectors!' was Sir Marcus Kimball, the Tory MP for Gainsborough, who has just retired as Chairman of the British Field Sports Society. A eulogistic statement from the Society recalls that since 1968 Sir Marcus has (single-handed, it is implied) defeated no fewer than sixteen Bills, twelve aimed at hare coursing, and one designed to ban stag hunting. 'One of Sir Marcus's greatest triumphs was the defeat of a Labour Bill to ban hare coursing in 1974-75,' the Society notes.

It continues: 'No sport is beyond his knowledge and skills. In 1950-52 he was joint master and huntsman of the Fitzwilliam Hounds . . . and he still hunts regularly. He also enjoys a considerable amount of fishing in the north of Scotland, he is a keen shooting man and is knowledgeable on falconry. His support for coursing is undoubted.'

In short there is no beast, on land, in the seas or up in the sky, no creature in fur, feathers or scales, which is safe from Sir Marcus's unending love of violent death. One wonders if, like the stag's head and antlers, the fox brushes, the stuffed pike, the glassy-eyed otters and the pathetic, terrified hares, he has case after case of dead Private Members' Bills mounted proudly on his wall.

I HAD TO FEEL sorry for Peter Fry, the 51-year-old Tory MP for Wellingborough. He was getting married to his second wife Helen a woman much younger and infinitely better-looking than himself. The ceremony was to take place in the House of Commons crypt, which is a splendid setting for any nuptials, and Fry and his bride were decked out in their most magnificent formal finery, walking through Westminster Hall towards the sacred moment. At this point they came upon Mr Speaker, George Thomas, escorting a group of Speakers from all over Europe who were paying a visit to our own Parliament. Glimpsing the happy couple, Mr Thomas brought his party to a halt and drew their attention to the delightful sight. 'Isn't it splendid,' he said, 'to see a father giving his daughter away like that!'

DENIS THATCHER watchers tell me that the Prime Minister's husband has begun to live up happily to his image. He has started to relish the fact that he has now become one of the Great Characters of English Fiction. Not the idea of himself as a henpecked ninny; as this column has reported before, Thatcher points out that he was a highly-paid businessman running important industries, and that these jobs do not go to incompetent fools. But he does rather enjoy the picture of himself as a jovial, convivial toper, a bit of a lad, combining a good head for strong drink with a sharp and cynical wit. Encountering the humorist William Rushton (himself no Tory) Thatcher remarked: 'When I'm not absolutely paralytic, I like to play a little golf!'

Here is another revealing story. Before the Falklands crisis blew up, Thatcher was dining at Chequers, and was placed next to Mr George Howard, the Chairman of the BBC. Denis was running through his usual (heart-felt) routine about the Beeb, staffed by pinkoes, disloyal crypto-Marxists, and so forth. Howard looked at him in a puzzled kind of way, and said: 'Thatcher, you're so far to the right, you're barely visible.'

The curious thing is that it is not Howard who tells this

story as a reflection on Thatcher, but Denis who tells it against Howard.

NOBODY WOULD EVER accuse Geoffrey Dickens, scourge of the paedophiles and Lothario of the *thé dansants*, of lying. On the other hand, it would be an equally bold fellow who went to the opposite extreme, and accused him of telling the truth. I leave readers to ponder in which category this tale falls.

According to Dickens, a constituent a farmer's wife, came to him with a sexual problem. She and her husband were incompatible. Dickens said that he would, if necessary, help with a doctor or, in the event of complete failure, a divorce lawyer.

A month or so later he met her again. With long face, she told him that she now had the opposite problem. Her husband had begun to make love to her too much. For example, the other day they had been looking at the chickens, and suddenly he had set upon her and had his way.

'That's fine, what's the problem?' inquired the solicitous MP.

'In Tesco's?' she allegedly asked.

What I say is: Pull the other one, Geoffrey.

I HAVE BEEN collecting Tam Dalyell stories. Tam, it will be remembered, is the MP for West Lothian, an old Etonian, former Chairman of the Cambridge University Conservative Association, and now probably the only Labour MP whose house is open to the public. He lives in a stately home called the Binns. Some people say Tam is a trifle loopy; others claim that he is mad. Certainly he is one of the half dozen most formidable and effective parliamentary fighters of the past ten years. Recently he has been unequivocally and stridently opposed to the Government's policy on the Falklands.

During an election he was campaigning with a Labour official. Canvassers who hope to complete their rounds are advised not to accept the many offers of tea they receive, especially from supporters of their own party.

Tam had turned down eight or ten such offers and had doggedly continued through his list right over lunch and tea time. Finally a sweet old lady offered him yet another cup.

'Yes,' said Tam suddenly, 'and we'll each take a boiled egg with it.' They got it, too.

Tam loves eggs. His vast consumption of them may account for the rather painful, strangulated manner of his speech. Taken to the canteen at the BBC in Scotland, he startled a lady behind the counter by producing two fresh eggs from his pocket and asking her to boil them.

The late John Mackintosh was also a Scottish Labour MP and something of a gourmet. One day he and his wife were invited round to the Binns for dinner, and looked forward with some pleasure to a fine baronial spread. Instead they were offered a single glass of sherry and a lot of conversation. Finally they were led into the dining-room, where the meal turned out to consist of scrambled eggs on toast. And no more sherry, either.

Another Labour MP made a speech near to the Binns, and went back with Tam to spend the night. Nothing was said about food until bedtime, when the famished legislator was shown down into the cellars. Tam swung open the door of a tall freezer, revealing an entire carcase of raw beef. 'If you get hungry,' he said, 'just cut yourself a steak off that.'

One of the most telling stories dates from shortly after his election. He was attending a conference at the Rob Roy Hotel in Aberfoyle when he got into a heated conversation with a girl who was a delegate from the Young Socialists. The dispute was about disarmament and it went on for some time.

About a quarter of an hour after it had ended, Dalyell suddenly lunged at the young woman with a fork, stabbing her in the arm. She spun round, grabbed the fork from his hand, and hurled it across the room.

'Ah-hah!' said Dalyell, 'so you do believe in defence!'

SPARE A KIND THOUGHT for poor Mr Reginald Eyre, the junior Minister of Transport, who made a diabolically bad speech about the future of Britain's railways. So distracted was he by his failure that he capped it by walking into the wrong division lobby, where he encountered the Labour Chief Whip, Mr Michael Cocks. 'My God, Reggie,' said the affable Cocks, 'I knew it wasn't a good speech, but I hadn't realised it was that bad!'

HERE'S A CURIOUS conundrum. There is a Tory MP called John Wells (no relation) who is a market gardener by trade. He grows exotic plants as a hobby. The other day Mrs Gail Jopling, helpmeet of the Government Chief Whip, held a Conservative Wives' Bazaar in London. Wells thoughtfully offered to contribute a number of rare and unusual plants which might be auctioned to raise money for the Conservatives' already bursting coffers. Among his gifts was a bizarre plant, reputed to have anti-aphrodisiac properties, a sort of vegetable version of

bromide. Wells clearly marked it as such when he sent the thing up for sale.

Somewhat to his surprise, bidding for this particular plant was extremely brisk. It was finally knocked down to Mrs Humphrey Atkins, wife of the former Lord Privy Seal, who resigned this year with Lord Carrington. I consider this a most remarkable tribute to a man who will be 60 this year.

MR GEORGE THOMAS, the Speaker, likes to run the Chamber with the same wary watchfulness as a boarding house landlady. The other day the Earl of Gowrie, who is a Northern Ireland Minister, felt the sharp lash of the Thomas tongue. Gowrie was lolling up in the peer's gallery overlooking the Commons chamber, with his feet casually propped up on the wooden rail in front.

The Speaker summoned a Government Whip. 'Who is that man?' he demanded, and the Whip told him. 'Well, go upstairs and tell him to take his feet off my furniture,' George instructed. The chastened Gowrie complied. It is to be hoped that, when he takes a bath at the House, he does not leave tell-tale rings around the side.

I HAVE BEEN pondering which member of the Cabinet is the least popular with the Prime Minister. Contrary to popular belief it is not—repeat not—John Nott. He has, after all, just won a tremendous victory, indirectly at least. This may not have commended him to the Service Chiefs, but it has certainly made his place in the Leader's throbbing bosom more secure. People say that he is scatter-brained and erratic, and so he is, but this is the whole charm of the man. You might as well criticise Michael Foot for being unkempt. And in any case she agrees with his defence policies.

It is sometimes thought that the most unloved must be Jim Prior, the Ulster Secretary, whose view of her is—once more—roughly that held by a greenfly for a ladybird. So great is their fractious animosity that Prior

after SHARAKU

actually had to ask her to stop Mr Ian Gow, her portly, glinting-spectacled Parliamentary Private Secretary, from going about encouraging people to filibuster his Northern Ireland Bill. This is a piece of legislation which, since it is opposed by both Mr Enoch Powell and Mr Charles Haughey, must be of almost Athenian wisdom. Short of thrusting Mr Foot to one side and attacking the Bill from the Opposition benches, there is not much more Mrs Thatcher could have done to make plain her dislike of its provisions.

I suspect, however, that the person squirming in the greatest disfavour now may well be Mr Francis Pym, the Foreign Secretary. She has always suspected him of having a wet, soggy, centre, and thoughout the Falklands crisis he let it be known to all and sundry, including the lamented Mr Haig, that he was keener on a negotiated settlement than she was. Things reached such a state that journalists who call at the Foreign Office to be briefed are asked not to sign in their names, a last desperate attempt by Pym to prevent the Thatcher Committee For Public Safety from gaining evidence with which to denounce him.

LIKE MOST PEOPLE I was delighted to see that Roy Jenkins had won the SDP leadership. It is said that he is a lazy man, and no doubt this is true, but that strikes me as a first-rate qualification for the job. Too many politicians, Margaret Thatcher and Tony Benn among them, work all the hours God sends. This is because they are under the absolute conviction that they know what is best for us. Jenkins takes the view that we all ought to be allowed to get on with whatever we want to do, whether making money or love. While he is taking a glass of Burgundy over an agreeable conversation with friends or playing a longish set of tennis, the others are summoning civil servants, drawing up blue-prints for our future, issuing speeches, directives and conspiracies; in short getting in our way.

In any case, Dr Owen appeared to have a very little idea

of what he wanted to do with the leadership had he won it. He even went round asking people how he ought to manage about the SDP if the voting had gone the other way. This is the equivalent of a man successfully persuading his inamorata to marry him, then not having the faintest idea of where to start on his wedding night.

The two men are not great friends, and were, I thought, distinctly ungenerous to each other after the result was declared. I suspect this was because both could claim the moral victory; Jenkins because he had won, Owen because he had gained far more votes than anyone had expected a month ago. Politicians tend to be magnanimous in victory only when the opposition has been humiliatingly crushed; when the loser can claim to have won, the resentment and annoyance continue to rankle.

Either way, the election revealed a pleasing and vulgar strain in the SDP. I was chatting to a member of the Steering Committee about which way he thought the members would vote. He explained that many would choose whichever candidate they had last heard at a public meeting. 'Frankly, our people are like baby ducklings,' he said. 'They will loyally follow the first thing which moves across their line of sight.'

An MP described the difficulties of persuading an electorate which is, to all intents, invisible, buried like a handful of pebbles strewn among the rest of the population. 'It's like pissing off the Grand Canyon. You assume you've hit something, but you've no idea where or what.'

TIME TO SALUTE Mr Denis Healey, Deputy Leader of the Labour Party and one of the doughtiest men in British politics. He was the Beachmaster at Anzio during the War, a job which, as far as I can gather, involved catching enemy shells as they landed and throwing them back. At the famous Walthamstowe by-election, which took place while he was Minister of Defence, he addressed a public meeting which was for the most part attended by members of the National Front. They booed and jeered and heckled him, shouting 'Communist', 'How much do the Russians pay you?' and the like. Other politicians, particularly those who have Special Branch protection, would have waited for their bodyguards to sort them out. Healey, however, jumped from the platform and smashed into the ringleader. He was pulled off only when his own police officer dragged him away in order to save the National Front yobbo from a well-deserved thrashing. It must be the only time the Branch has had to protect a crazed attacker from a politician.

Intriguingly, none of the National Front thicks were charged with anything. This is, because the Secretary of State would have had to appear in court to give evidence of his own part in the affray.

Mr Healey's boundless energy and enthusiasm were displayed more recently at a by-election in Glasgow. He is a great one for touring pubs, where, he reckons, he is able to relax at ease with the voters. In one bar he fell into converse with a deaf and dumb woman who, unknown to the Deputy Leader, was a prostitute. The various local Labour people with him knew this very well, and watched in some disquiet as she propositioned him in deaf-and-dumb language. Finally, as this bizarre silent chat continued, a senior Labour official elbowed her way in and said, 'C'mon Denis, give us a song.' So he abandoned the young woman and sat down at the piano, where he sang 'On Ilkla' Moor Baht Hat' at the top of his voice. The mute prostitute was so impressed that she made a cash contribution to Labour Party funds.

I SEE THAT the House of Commons hairdresser has had to advertise for custom. I am surprised. The best advertisements are his haircuts, which offer value for money not commonly seen these days. For only 90 pence, he will cut off twice as much hair as Vidal Sassoon does for £25. MPs who have just left the salon, situated in a dark corridor near to Annie's Bar, are immediately recognisable by their splendid coiffure, a sort of cross between a Prussian subaltern and Sid Vicious. When you get your hair cut in the Commons, it stays cut.

It is a fitting tribute to the tonsorial skills manifested there that the women who work at the House, MPs, secretaries and so on, have asked for their own hairdresser. This has been refused on the grounds that there would not be enough demand. I suspect this was not true; in fact, the MPs who run the Services Committee were terrified that the secretaries would spend all their days under the drier, instead of getting on with typing their tedious and self-important letters.

EDWARD HEATH LAST spoke to Margaret Thatcher in early 1982, at a reception in the Carlton Club held to mark the unveiling of a new portrait of her. He said 'Good evening.' She said nothing at all. After he had been similarly snubbed by two other party grandees he walked out in a huff. There is no love lost between them whatsoever. Theirs has become one of the great, classic feuds.

People often inquire whether Heath genuinely hates the Prime Minister, or whether he simply believes that her policies are wrecking the country. The answer is both. He regards her as arrogant, wilful and traitorous. He is deeply and bitterly resentful of the way that she and her friends have reviled the 1970–74 Heath Government of which they were prominent members—just as the real dislike among Labour leaders for Tony Benn is for his denunciation of the 1974–79 Government.

Yet this fury is not really typical of the new Heath. The formerly aloof party leader, capable of deeply wounding a trusted colleague with a cutting remark, has gone. In its place there is a far more relaxed and amiable and energetic man. The secret of this startling change is his recovery from a serious and long undetected illness.

For years he had been suffering from an underactive thyroid. The symptoms include lassitude, lack of concentration, irritability, and the disquieting habit of falling asleep without warning. Some of his colleagues now say that they could detect the first signs during his spell as Prime Minister; his mind would wander off during important meetings, or he would look unexpectedly drowsy. The illness is progressive but slow, so that friends, and even his own doctor, did not notice how severe it was becoming. He began to fall asleep at concerts and dinner parties; once he dropped off while talking to Henry Kissinger. Aides would mutter vaguely that he had been working too hard. The stories soon percolated through Westminster where it was whispered that he had been eating and drinking too much.

Finally, in March last year, his doctor agreed to a second opinion and he was examined by Sir Richard Bayliss, the Queen's physician. Bayliss diagnosed the illness, prescribed a course of drugs, and Heath—after a spell of convalescence at a Torquay hotel—recovered fairly rapidly.

Now his celebrated chilly remarks have been replaced by self-deprecatory humour. Earlier this year he gave a surprise party for two friends who had just married. One of the guests was Sir George Young, who had just been appointed (to a chorus of abuse from those who normally serve as the Downing Street hit-squad) race relations Minister. 'Ah, the second most unpopular man in the Tory Party!' Heath beamed when Sir George walked in. Not the most dazzling of drolleries, but a world away from the old Heath.

The bitterness towards Margaret Thatcher is deep and probably unchangeable. The new Heath's opinion of the Prime Minister has not mellowed one bit. He thought her a second-rate Cabinet Minister, and would have liked to drop her from his shadow cabinet after his defeat; instead he humiliated her in March 1974 by making her number two to Robert Carr in the Treasury team. When she took over in 1975 she began the process of revenge by kicking Carr upstairs to the Lords.

As with all good vendettas, attempts to end it only make things worse. After a trip to the Middle East, he was invited round to Mrs Thatcher's house to brief her. According to him, she wasn't interested in what he had to say. 'All I heard was her views, not mine!' he said. But according to her people, he offended her by giving her a child's lecture on the area, along 'now this place is Egypt' lines. At one point she expressed admiration for President Assad. Afterwards he said grumpily, 'I could only think that Assad had mad eyes, like Keith Joseph.' Either way, the meeting was a fiasco.

He hoped—perhaps a bit too openly for his own good—that if the Tories won the 1979 election with a slender majority he might become Foreign Secretary, as a sort of good-conduct pass for the Tory left-wing. But on the Friday night the new Prime Minister, her deputy, Mr Whitelaw, and her Chief Whip, Humphrey Atkins, met for dinner and quickly decided that he should be left out. So at 7.30 on the Saturday morning, an official car set out from Downing Street for the Wiltshire house where Heath was weekending. Its only passenger was a letter in which the new Prime Minister said briefly that she had appointed Peter Carrington to the post Heath had hoped for. The letter contained no reference to Heath himself.

Her suggestion that he go to Washington as British Ambassador came a month later. 'It was such an obvious, silly ploy,' says a Heath friend. 'You offer him a job you know he can't possibly accept, so it looks as if he's the sulky one.' Thatcher people say it was a genuine attempt to find a role for a world statesman. Heath's side say that proves they are even stupider: 'How could you have an ambassador in the United States who entirely disagrees with Government policy? You couldn't trust a word he sent back.'

Heath is now disliked, mistrusted and resented by very many Tories. His frequent and bitter attacks on the Government are seen as gross disloyalty. He is compared unfavourably with Home, who went quietly, without fuss, and with Macmillan, whose own strictures on Mrs Thatcher are delivered in an elliptical ironic code which Tories find acceptable. There is a strong suspicion that Heath is relishing a sweet revenge, at whatever cost to the party, and there is certainly some truth in this. He clearly derives deep personal satisfaction from finding means and excuses for attacking her.

159

Some of his friends are quite aggressive about this. 'Listen,' one of them said recently, 'Ted led the party for ten years and was Prime Minister for four. If he thinks that the country is being destroyed, he has every bloody right to say so.' The row is now so heated and personal that both leaders tend to measure the loyalty of their friends by the strength of their antipathy to the other.

Matters are also confused by his sense of humour, which even today can be baffling to onlookers. At Hillhead, while canvassing for the Tory candidate, he cheerfully agreed that his own economic policies were the same as Roy Jenkins's. 'What a kick in the teeth for our candidate,' says a Thatcher loyalist MP. 'Ah, Ted's impish sense of humour again,' says a friend.

Heath is no fool, and he doesn't see the remotest chance of his leading the Tories again. Nor is he running through an elaborate game plan, designed to let him sidle back into power.

What he does believe, however, is that a confused result in the next election might bring him back into the Cabinet. He has no intention of joining the Social Democrats, who have, he thinks, too strong a socialist leaning for comfort. But he has said in public that if the next election forced an accommodation between the Tories and the SDP, he would be willing to serve. And, though he doesn't mention this, everyone knows that the first condition made by the SDP would be the swift disposal of Heath's greatest political enemy. With her out of the way, who could resist the demands to find work once again for Britain's best-known unemployed man of destiny?